humorous monologues

humorous monologues

by
Vernon Howard

illustrated by Audrey E. Wichern

PLAYERS PRESS
P. O. Box 1132
Studio City, California

humorous monologues

Simultaneously Published in:
Australia, Canada, U.K., U. S. A.
Printed in the U.S.A.

Library of Congress Cataloging-in-Publication Data

Howard, Vernon Linwood, 1918-
    Humorous monologues / by Vernon Howard ; illustrated by Audrey E. Witchern.
        p. cm
    ISBN 0-88734-667-7 (alk. paper)
        1. Monologues. 2. Acting. I. Title.
    PN2080 .H66 2000
    812'.54--dc21   00-060610

TABLE OF CONTENTS

humorous
monologues

HOW TO USE THIS BOOK

Anyone can perform the monologues in this book—young folks or adults. Monologues have long been a favorite type of dramatic entertainment, because they provide hilarity at the party, in the club, camp, and schoolroom, and at social gatherings of all kinds and descriptions. They also provide a practical and wholesome outlet for pent-up dramatic abilities or unsuspected talents. Monologues may be presented individually or a festival of monologues might be staged with a group of volunteers performing on the same stage.

This book was especially written to provide easy material for those who have had little or no experience with this lively form of dramatic art. The following ideas and suggestions are specifically listed to make *your* performance easy—and funny!

Selecting your material: You have a wide choice of pieces in this collection. Go through the pages and select one that appeals to you in particular. Choose one that you can handle with ease. Get familiar with its feeling by reading it several times. Before long you will begin to picture yourself in the role.

Some of the monologues are suitable for performers of either sex. In some the character's name only needs to be changed to fit.

Some of the monologues call for double roles. There is extra humor as you make swift changes from one character to another. These changes can be effected in a number of ways, such as switching from a male to a female hat, by speaking in a low voice as a boy and a high voice as a girl, or by simply shifting physical positions back and forth.

Many audiences find something especially funny about a boy taking a girl's role and vice versa. If you keep your natural voice while acting an opposite-sex role, this sometimes adds to the humor, sometimes detracts. Choose a monologue that *you* can get the most humor and feeling out of.

Memorizing the monologue: Read the whole text aloud once or twice. Next, memorize three or four sentences at a time. Get to know them before proceeding to further sections. Speak them aloud with gestures, facial expressions, voice inflections, for this will help you to remember them. Carefully follow the directions for pausing, frowning, looking sad, and so forth. Remember to emphasize where emphasis is indicated, and to pause when paragraphs or dots in the text indicate a break. When you are asking a question be sure to make it very clear that it *is* a question. You will be delighted to see how quickly the routine becomes natural to you.

Rehearsal: Once you have the monologue more or less in mind, you are ready for an informal rehearsal. Go off by yourself. Stand before a mirror as you rehearse and try to see yourself as others will see you. Then, stand in the center of the room and imagine yourself delivering (or actually deliver) your monologue with an imaginary audience. Imitate some of the stage or television professionals you may have seen. Make corrections and improvements as you proceed. You will find yourself almost automatically changing things for the better, and even developing your own style.

Next, try it out on your family. Don't be afraid to ask for comments and suggestions. Again go through the routine with their ideas in mind. Now you're almost ready.

Costume: Most of the pieces can be delivered in everyday dress. However, a touch of oddness in your clothing will add to the fun. You might wear a straw hat decorated with flowers or carry an open umbrella or wear a pair of huge cardboard eyeglasses. For roles that call for a specific costume, you can dress accordingly. A small child might wear a bright hair ribbon and carry a lollipop. You can turn your imagination loose with some lively results.

Setting: In most monologues, no particular background is needed. Of course a few background properties will help to establish a gay mood. In the monologue, *Look, George,* an art gallery could be indicated by hanging a few pictures; in *Complaint Desk,* the performer could sit behind a desk labeled as such. Enough room should be provided to allow the freedom of movement that the monologue requires.

You don't need a stage, but a raised platform is a help. If you have no platform, clear a fairly wide space in front of you and let your audience set in a half-circle around you.

Atmosphere can also be created by having background music. A phonograph could be operated by a friend, or a live musician could play gay tunes, sad refrains, and other types of music in keeping with the mood of the monologue. The instrument or musician should play off-stage or off to one side. Of course the speaker should always be clearly heard above the music.

Your introduction: A guest may introduce you to the audience—"Let me now present Mr. Eddie Greenhorn, who will tell us of the origins of many of our famous proverbs"—or, you may simply introduce yourself.

Your performance: The *best* way to do it is *simply* to do it! Remember, your audience is probably relaxed and in a *mood to laugh.* Take advantage of this and even the tiniest joke or gesture —or even a mistake!—may bring howls of mirth. Laughter is your main object! Enter briskly, take immediate command of the situation, speak boldly and confidently. Never give a hint of apology in word or expression. Forget who you are—*imagine that you are actually the character you are portraying.*

Make believe you're talking to someone in the back row. Your voice need be no louder than that. If guests are informally seated about you, speak to the tops of their heads. Don't look anyone directly in the eye. Speak clearly, make your gestures broad so that they are easily understood. Stay in full view of the audience and, when possible, keep your face or profile toward them. Don't be stiff—move your head and body.

Exaggeration plays an important part in comedy. When you scowl, scowl fiercely; when you droop, droop as if you are about to collapse. Use all of your natural means to convey the feeling. For example, surprise can be comically indicated by a gaping mouth, staring eyes, a stiff pose. Remember that distance dims eyesight.

Most of the monologues in this book are also suitable for simple reading aloud to an audience. Lots of chuckles can be produced by assuming the role just as if you were delivering it from memory. In this case you can explain the character and situation to the listeners. Hold the book to one side, so it is not between you and your audience. Look at it when you need to, not continuously. Look up from the book as you supply the gestures. The piece should be read with all the usual gestures and inflections. You might wish to deliver your first monologues by the reading method. As you gain experience and familiarity with dramatics, you'll want to perform from memory more and more often.

Your first performances are worth their weight in experience. Analyze them, try to make the funny spots even funnier. Go over the weak sections to see how they might be improved. Don't hesitate to ask a few friends how they think the piece could be made funnier.

Let the audience enjoy a full laugh at a funny line. Do not proceed to the next line until you are certain they will hear it. If a laugh fails to come when you expect it, calmly proceed as if you really didn't expect laughter. (Or hold your cupped hand to your ear, as if asking for a titter.) You may also hear laughter when you least expect it; if so, pause. As you grow more familiar with audience reactions you will be able to judge your timing more accurately.

TROUBLE WITH A DOG

Character: Female (or male) on phone.

Hello, hello . . . operator? Will you connect me with the **city** dog pound? *Which* city dog pound? *This* city dog pound . . . Yes, the place where they keep stolen dogs. No, I did *not* steal a dog. I want to see if they've found Miss Fifi. You have **no** listing for a Miss Fifi? Of course not; Miss Fifi is a dog . . . **a** *dog* . . . that's spelled d-o . . . d-o . . . operator, can't you **spell** *dog*? . . . Now, will you please get me the pound? What's that, you want to tell me a little joke? Well, go ahead. Since the city dog pound is so little they call it the dog *ounce?* . . . Very funny, operator, but I still want the dog ounce . . . I mean . . . operator, *please!* What's that number again? *Airedale six-six-three-three* and ask for Mr. Cocker Q. Spaniel? Thank you, operator.

Hello, is this the city dog pound? What's that? An *ounce* . . . I've heard it before, sir, so will you please just inform me if you have a Miss Fifi there? You once knew a Fifi but she moved **to** Paris? Everyone's a comedian these days . . . Look, I'd just like to know if you have my dog there. You see, a mad dog chased Miss Fifi down the alley. How do *I* know what made the dog mad? . . . Anyway, this mad dog chased Miss Fifi down an alley . . . or maybe it was *up* an alley . . . What *kind* of a dog chased her? I think it was a St. Bernard which is very disappointing because if you can't trust a St. Bernard whom *can* you trust?

What's that, you'd like a description? Well, I'm five feet four, weigh one-hundred and twenty, and am unmarried . . . Oh, you mean Miss Fifi. She's eight inches tall, weighs fifteen pounds and has been married five times—three water spaniels and two French poodles . . . Her color? When clean she's white with black spots, when dirty she's black with white spots . . . When she's mad her eyes turn an angry lavender. Oh, yes, and every Thursday she turns purple . . . What's strange about that—

every Thursday the neighbor boy sneaks over with his water colors. Craziest sight you ever saw . . .

What kind of a temper does Miss Fifi have? Well, it's not exactly *even*. To be perfectly honest, she does sometimes bite a little. But the scars usually heal very quickly . . . Yes, she does take an occasional nip at house-to-house salesmen. But they just smile, wave, and limp merrily away . . . Of course sometimes she becomes very stubborn. Like the time I told her to get off the kitchen table . . . Or the time I told her to sleep in her own bed . . . Or the time I told her I was perfectly capable of driving the car by myself.

What's that—you think you have something there that answers Miss Fifi's description—except that it's a cat? . . . You really *do* think you have Miss Fifi there? Fine! There's only one way to make sure, though. Just offer her a bone and see what she does. Go ahead, I'll wait for you . . . Hello, did you offer her a bone? What happened? She bit you on the second finger? I'm *so* sorry; that couldn't be Miss Fifi; she always bites the *third* finger . . . You'd like to do *what?* But wouldn't a dog look funny walking down the street in two parts?

Well, if you can't find Miss Fifi, maybe you have some other dog for me. What breeds do you have? Spaniels, setters, terriers, holsteins . . . but isn't a *holstein* a *cow?* You know that it's a cow but you like to hear an occasional *moo* around there? . . . What's that—if I come on down you'll give me a glass of skim milk and three pounds of butter?

But tell me about your Boston terriers. What's that—they've all moved to Philadelphia? . . . *Very* funny. And I suppose your German shepherds have all moved to England? Oh, Alaska . . . tell me, do you have a Great Dane? I *didn't* ask if you had a *great brain* . . . I doubt if you have one at all. Do you have a beagle? You haven't seen a beagle since you last owned a fifty-cent piece? . . . Look, I'm not talking about birds. I'll give you just one more chance . . . do you have a boxer? You do? What's he like? He's won his last six fights by knockouts?

What I really want is a watchdog. No, I won't take any kind of a dog and tie my wristwatch to him . . . Tell me, does a pointer make a good watchdog? It does? Why won't you let me have it . . . because it's rude to point? . . . You say the strangest things. Tell me, do you have a Mexican hairless there? No? They're all in Mexico looking for their hair?

Please, won't you take another look for Miss Fifi? . . . How does she bark? Mostly with her mouth . . . What does it sound like? Like something awful.

Wait a minute! I hear something! Just a second while I look out the window . . . yes, yes, it's Miss Fifi . . . she's come home all by herself . . . wait a minute, not quite all by herself. Wow! Six Fifi's—one big and five little. Mama Fifi and her five little Fifi's! Thank you, for being so kind. Goodbye! Here Fifi, here Fifi, here . . . oh, the whole pack of you—come to dinner!

MY FIRST FOOTBALL GAME

Character: Teen-age girl.

Shall I tell you about the very first football game I ever saw? Of course I didn't see it very well because Harry couldn't afford very good seats. In fact the seats we got were so far back we found it better to sit on a very sturdy branch that grew over the edge of the stadium . . . But even this was crowded. I was constantly moving over to make room for others up there: Six crows and three red-headed woodpeckers.

I must admit that Harry did everything possible for my comfort. We had popcorn, peanuts, hot dogs, ice cream bars. Best of all, Harry promised to pay me back the very next day . . .

Harry taught me the idea of the game. A man has to carry the football from one end of the field to the other. Isn't that a perfectly silly thing to make a *game* out of? . . . But there they were—full grown men running, falling, kicking all over the place just to have the ball for a few seconds . . . Why, they could have saved their money so *each* player had one.

My biggest confusion came when I tried to tell *our* team from the enemy team. Harry said that our team was the one with the football. But pretty soon the other team had the ball and I was all confused again.

One time I looked down and there was a player carrying a bass drum instead of a football. I asked Harry about it and he said it was the half. Well, it certainly looked like a *whole drum* to me . . . Then it was the musicians' turn to play. Of course they didn't play football . . . they played *music* . . . I guess someone had kicked the football over the fence because all the players were gone quite a while looking for it. But pretty soon they found it and the players came whooping back again.

I asked Harry why all the players got in a big secret huddle just before each play. He looked at me kind of funny. But when I begged and begged he finally broke down and told me what the big mystery was. It seems that the enemy team was planning to play a dirty trick on ours. They were trying to plant fifty tons of dynamite down in a corner of the field. Then they were going to try and lead our team over the buried dynamite and boom! the game would be over . . . I asked Harry if that was strictly according to the rules but he just smiled mysteriously and said nothing. Funny thing, though, as much as the teams plotted to blow each other up, nothing ever happened . . . This little incident certainly made me look up to Harry. He was the only one there who knew the secret. He knows just about *everything!* And he tells it all to little old *me*!

He even explained to me about the men with the striped shirts. They were afraid of football and just stood off to one side and played their own little game—whistle blowing. Every time a player fell down with the ball these funny little men blew their whistles like mad and made crazy little motions with their arms. Harry said it was all part of the game.

I finally got the game figured out. You see, each player has a number on his back. If player number 67 catches the ball his team scores 67 points; while if player number 88 catches the ball his team scores 88 points. Somehow this doesn't seem fair to players with little numbers like 12 and 15, does it? . . . It was an exciting game all the way. The final score was five-thousand, nine hundred and thirty-five to zero.

THE WILD, WILD WEST

Character: Cowboys fighting a duel (double role).

(Gus, hand on holster) I'm going to plug you, Saddlebag Sam.

(Sam, hand on holster) I'm filling you with lead, Gunsmoke Gus.

(Gus) You coyote.

(Sam) You rattlesnake.

(Gus) You no-good cattle-rustler.

(Sam) You no-no-good horse thief.

(Gus, taking a step) I'm coming for you, Sam.

(Sam, taking a step) I'm heading for you, Gus.

(Gus) Take a last look at the sunrise, Sam.

(Sam) It happens to be sunset, Gus.

(Gus) Don't tell me I don't know sunrise from sunset, Sam.

(Sam) Don't tell me I don't know sunset from sunrise, Gus.

(Gus) You're going to taste lead, Sam.

(Sam) Too early for dinner, Gus.

(Gus, stepping forward) I'm coming, Sam.

(Sam, stepping forward) Me, too, Gus.

(Gus) You're a copycat, Sam.

(Sam) You're a polecat, Gus.

(Gus) Say your last word, Sam.

(Sam) Speak your last piece, Gus.

(Gus) Never was much for talking, Sam.

(Sam) Me neither, Gus.

(Gus) Ready, Sam?

(Sam) Ready, Gus.

(Gus, shooting) Bang, Sam.

(Sam, shooting) Bang, Gus.

(Gus) You're a bad shot, Sam.

(Sam) You, too, Gus.

(Gus) Have a glass of buttermilk with me, Sam?

(Sam) Sure thing, Gus.

HOW?

Character: A book lecturer (male or female).

(Enter with several books and a list) Good evening, ladies and gentlemen. My name is Bookbug Binder. I am editor of the How Publishing Company. As you know, we publish books on *how* to do things. I would like to read you the list of our latest publications. For you nature lovers we have a number of new titles . . . (read from list)

How to Tell a Butterfly from a Dish of Butter.

How to Make a Wool Dress for a Cotton Boll-Weevil.

How to Stay Dry While Sitting Beneath a Weeping Willow.

How to Entertain a Leopard.

How to Get Away from a Leopard Who Isn't Entertained.

I'm sure you nature lovers will be delighted with our little list. These books sell for five dollars apiece—two for three dollars . . . We set this odd price just to confuse you. Oh, yes, these nature books are authentically illustrated by a trained seal . . . Our next list is for you folks who love to travel. Listen to these moving titles . . . (read from list)

How I Lived Ninety Years in China, by Wun Sun Ho.

How Could You Live So Long? by *Mrs.* Wun Sun Ho.

How to Swim the Pacific Ocean.

How to Make Friends with Sharks.

How to Get to France on a Five-Dollar Bill

How to Get There on a *Boat.*

How to Go to the North Pole.

How to Keep Your Tootsies from Freezing.

You may obtain these books from our shop any time after dark . . . I say this for your own protection—anyone seeing you buy them might think you a little odd . . . Ah! Our next little list of newly published titles is for you folks who like handicrafts . . . (read from list)

How to Work with Your Hands.

How to Work with Your Feet If You Have Clumsy Hands.

How to Build a Six-Car Garage.

How to Get Six Cars.

How to Build Almost Anything.

How to Tear Down Most of It.

How to Install Your Own Plumbing System.

How to Call for the Nearest Plumber.

All of these books are exactly three hundred pages long, and cost three dollars. If you can't afford more than two dollars we'll gladly tear out one-hundred pages.

We also have a new series of new books that are very new. Actually, they're *not* new, since they were originally scratched on rocks by a cave-man. But we call them new to compete with other publishers. Listen to the titles. (read from list)

How to Eat Soup with Your Fingers.

How to Ignore Folks Who Call You a Pig.

How to Be a Perfect Gentleman.

How to Be a Perfect Lady in Case You're Not a Gentleman.

How to Attract Attention at a Party.

How to Get Back Down from the Ceiling.

How to Be Popular.

How to Be Repulsive in Case You'd Rather.

How to Walk with Grace and Dignity.

How to Walk with Jane and Susie.

How to Make People Like You.

How to Stop Twisting Their Arms.

You can have the whole lot for fifty cents. If you don't want the books, just give me fifty cents anyway, to show your good manners.

Lastly, we have some splendid *how-to* books. (read from list)

How to Be a Bullfighter.

How to Remove Horns from Your Back.

How to Be Happy Though Miserable.

How to Be Miserable Though Happy.

How to Sing at Midnight.

How to Get Out of Town Fast.

How to Imitate a Mouse.

How to Avoid Mouse Traps.

How Many Times Must I Tell You to Stay Out of the Cookie Jar?

How Do You Do?

If you want copies of these titles, better get your order in right away . . . they're going like crazy. There's said to be a fuel shortage!

OUR NATIONAL SPORTS

Character: An athlete (male or female).

Would you like to hear how some of our national sports and pastimes were started? No? Well, you're stuck anyway.

The running broad jump was first introduced in America by a man named Springer B. Leap. It seems Mr. Leap came home one day and found a big water puddle between the sidewalk and porch. So he did just what you and I would do under the circumstances. He walked around it . . . He later invented the running broad jump.

Baseball was created as a result of a number of confusing circumstances. It was first call Faceball and consisted of Pilgrims throwing pumpkin pies at Indians on Thanksgiving Day . . . When the Indians, in turn, chased the Pilgrims, it was called Chaseball . . . The Pilgrim ladies retaliated by throwing household items at the Indians, after which it was called Vaseball . . . But the Indians and Pilgrims finally got together in peace and decided to rename the sport. They called it Baseball in honor of Robert T. Base, who had held the coats of both teams.

It's hardly worth mentioning, but handball is so named because the ball used for this game is usually shaped like a hand . . . When the ball is shaped like a foot, it is called football . . .

Swimming is an ancient sport that was first created by a caveman named Wiglag. It isn't well known, but one day Wiglag was walking along the river when his wife suddenly pushed him in. "That's for not buying me a new dinosaur coat," she screamed . . . Poor Wiglag floated on top of the water for hours, desperately wishing that he would drown. But since he didn't sink, he called to his fellow cave men in sign language. As he moved his arms about, he found himself moving on top of the water. His experience created such a great interest in water, it wasn't long before mankind learned to swim. As I say, this story—though true—isn't well known.

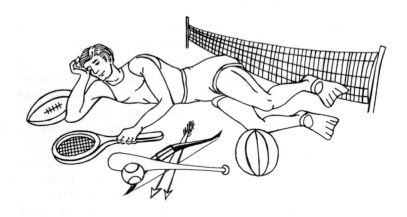

Pole vaulting was invented by an ancient Roman soldier who had overstayed his leave. Taking a long spear he vaulted smack into the second floor of the barracks . . . Unfortunately for him, the general was holding a midnight inspection and the soldier plopped right on top of him. However, the soldier's ingenuity so intrigued the general that he ordered all soldiers henceforth to pole vault into the barracks. This was the beginning of aerial warfare.

Hurdle races were first performed in ancient Egypt. Desert travelers found it necessary to jump over the pyramids that stood in the way . . . Needless to say, those Egyptians were much better hurdlers than our modern athletes.

Tennis was created by a pair of fishermen who had a big fight over a fish net. Each stood on a side of the net and tossed a week-old herring back and forth at each other . . . They decided after a while that since they had to fight they might as well make it interesting. So instead of a herring they tossed codfish balls . . . But codfish balls had a tendency to muss up the face after a particularly accurate toss. So they then used peaches. When they got tired of peach jam . . . well, it was just a short step to fuzzy tennis balls.

The indoor game of Chinese Checkers was created in a supermarket. Between checking out groceries, two clerks played a harmless little game with marbles and a board. The Boss came along, saw what they were doing and remarked, "Looks like Chinese to me, you checkers." And so the game was named.

The relay race was created when a squad of Greek soldiers accidentally came upon a live hand grenade. Having nothing else to do, they just ran around and passed it around to each other . . . Today, there is a bronze statue in Greece dedicated to the memory of these four clever soldiers.

The Indians are credited with inventing the bow and arrow. But really they didn't quite know what to do with it. They weren't sure whether to shoot the arrow from the bow or the bow from the arrow . . . So they tossed a coin for it, an Indian head penny.

The game of Drop the Handkerchief was first started by a woman of ancient Mesopotamia who dropped her handkerchief to catch the attention of a passing shepherd. When the shepherd saw that it was a much better handkerchief than his own he pocketed it and promptly forgot all about the woman.

And finally, the game of water polo was started by the famous Venetian adventurer, Marco Polo. One day Marco was leaning over the side of a ship and looking thoughtfully at the great expanse of blue below him. One of the crew saw him and said in passing, "That's water, Polo." The name has stuck ever since.

If you wish to know the origin of other kinds of sports, just ask Ed Jones . . . (substitute name of prominent local person for Ed Jones) He's a great sport!

LEFT TURN

Character: Driving instructor (male or female) to female pupil.

That's right, ma'am, just relax . . . we'll have you driving this car in no time . . . now, the first thing to do is sit in the driver's seat of this dual control car. Nothing can go wrong . . . no, no, don't sit on me . . . wait till I move over . . . that's right. All right, the next thing to do is turn the motor over . . . no, no, not with your hands . . . just press this little button. That's it. Now gently let the car ease forward . . . (jerk violently, shout) I said *gently!* Well, we're on the way. Remember, if you want to stop, just gently apply your brakes . . . no, a tree will *not* do just as well. Watch out for that truck over there. *Why?* (exasperated) Well, maybe he's a new driver . . .

Let me show you proper signals. Straight out for a left turn . . . that's right . . . (shout) Your arm, *not your foot!* . . . Up for right and down for stop, that's right. No, ma'am, you may *not* just wave wildly and let them take their choice . . . No, we have no signal for waving to a good-looking man in the next car. You are going ten miles an hour—speed up a little . . . no, ma'am, *ninety* is not a *little.* Now slow down—a little at a time . . . (jerk forward)

Be careful, we're coming to a tunnel. Don't worry, there *is* an opening there. Careful, now . . . (shout) Please, lady, *open your eyes!* Look, see that big black spot ahead . . .? That's the tunnel. No, you won't need a compass to guide you . . . Here we are, in the tunnel. Don't be frightened, there are rarely any bears in here. Nothing to frighten you . . .

The next thing to learn is how to go around corners. See that corner coming up? I want you to make a right turn. Turn the wheel . . . (shout) no, the *other way!* . . . That's right. Now, make a turn here and watch out for that hardware store . . . Careful . . . Well, that's wasn't *too* bad but we'll have to return those rakes and shovels that got caught in the bumper.

Let's take up street signals. No, I don't mean we're going to dig them up . . . Just study them. Remember, a red signal means *stop* and a green one means *go*. I'm sorry you don't like those colors. You'd like *purple* for stop and *blue* for go?

See that white line in the middle of the road? Be sure you stay on this side of it. I know there are cars on the other side . . . but if you look very closely, you'll see that they're *going the other way*. Yes, when we come back *you* can have that side—it's all fair and square. No, the white line is not for motorcycles . . . Just keep thinking to yourself, *my* side, *his* side, *my* side, *his* side.

I hear a police siren. Pull over to the curb and stop. That's it. (quickly) No, no, it's not necessary to bow as they go by.

Remember to keep your eyes open for traffic signs. See those over there . . . thirty mile limit . . . slow, curve ahead . . . railroad crossing . . . see if you can read a few . . . Joe's Hot Dogs . . . Eggs For Sale . . . well, that's the *general* idea . . . be sure to watch for signs that say *curves ahead*. No, there won't be any that say *curves behind*. And be extra careful for animals that might dart across the road . . . you know, dogs, cats, rabbits . . . no, it's not likely that you'll see an alligator . . .

Do you think you can drive back to town without help? You can? Fine! Just a minute while I put on this blindfold . . . *Why?* Oh, I just think I'll feel better that way.

ORDER, PLEASE

Character: Girl at expensive restaurant with boy friend.

Oh, Wilbur, it was so nice of you to bring me here to the Ritz-de-Paris for dinner. I didn't *dream* that you'd take my hint so soon . . . after all, I only asked you three times last week . . . What's that, you've been wanting to take me here for a long time but couldn't find anyone to sell your car to? . . . Oh, Wilbur, why would you have to sell your car in order to bring me here? I'll know when the check comes . . . ?

(Dreamy) Oh, Wilbur, isn't everything so rich and romantic . . .? Just listen to that twenty-piece orchestra! Do you know what tune they're playing? No, I don't think it's called, You're My Million Dollar Girl Friend . . . what? You think they *will* play that before the evening's over? You say the wittiest things, Wilbur! Don't you just adore this smooth Parisian atmosphere? Can't you just see the Eiffel Tower, the Rue de Paree, the River Seine . . .? . . . you wish you could see the First National Bank of Paris? Oh, look, here comes our waiter. I hope his name is Pierre . . . my whole evening is spoiled if I can't call him *Pierre.* I'll just ask him . . . (to waiter) Waiter, is your name Pierre? (disappointed) Oh . . . Well, could we *call* you Pierre . . .? On one condition? What is it? (gushily to Wilbur) Wilbur, you're a dear for tipping him just so we can call him Pierre! What do you mean, it would have been much cheaper just to call him *Joe?*

Oh, here's the menu . . . (look at menu, happily mutter to self) Pheasant under glass, nineteen-fifty . . . What Wilbur, you'd rather have it under a plain old piece of wood? Look at this—New York fillet . . . twelve-seventy-five. What, Wilbur, there's a nice Santa Fe steak for only six-fifty? I know what I'll have—a tenderloin with French fried onions . . . No, Wilbur, I will *not* have a hot dog with American fried onions . . . Why are you taking out your wallet? Oh, you just want to flash your five

dollar bill around to impress everyone . . . (gushy) You're *so* dashing and debonair.

What would *you* like, Wilbur? (amazed) What do you mean, *go?* . . . But Wilbur, this is the fanciest place in town—we've only been here ten minutes. Isn't it *wonderful?* To think that poor little old you and I would come here . . . what's that, I can say that again with emphasis on the *poor* little old *you?* Well, if it seems expensive just remember that you only live once . . . what's that, you're ready to die *anytime?*

Look, here come our salads . . . (surprised) But how come there's just *one* salad with *two* forks? (in romantic ecstasy) Oh, you think it would be romantic if we *shared together* . . . you're *so* romantic . . .

Ah, here are our steaks! (look at plate, frown) Wilbur, how come this steak looks exactly like macaroni and cheese? Oh, French steaks *always* look like macaroni and cheese . . . (taste it) Funny, but it also *tastes* like macaroni and cheese . . . these French cafes are certainly *different* . . .

Look, Wilbur, here come some celebrities! There's the president of the Montana Railroad who makes eighty-thousand a year . . . the vice-president of Apex Steel who makes ninety-thousand a year . . . what's that, Wilbur, take a good look at the president of the Jaloppy Club who makes *forty-seven a week?* . . . Isn't it thrilling watching all these rich and handsome men come in? What? . . . you think it would be more thrilling watching a poor and ugly boy go *out?*

Listen, they're playing *our* song! No, it is *not* called Let's Sneak Out the Back Door When the Waiter's Not Looking . . . Look, here comes a gypsy violinist to play at our table . . . (dreamily sway to music) Isn't it romantic . . .? (surprised) Wilbur, it is not considered courteous to kick a gypsy in the shins!

(Sigh with contentment) Oh, Wilbur, what a lovely meal. And it was *so* different . . . steaks that taste like macaroni and cheese, shrimp salad that tastes like water cress and French pastry that tastes like stale bread . . . my, but these French cooks are clever . . . What's that—you're clever, *too?*

Well, here comes the check—better get out your wallet . . . (surprised) Wilbur, why are you whispering to the waiter . . .? (alarmed) And why is he punching you in the nose? (indignant) Come, Wilbur, I won't allow you to slump there and be insulted . . . Let's get out of this crude place. Believe me, Wilbur, I won't ask you ever to take me to this joint again . . . Imagine! . . . socking you in the nose just because you whispered in his ear. What's that, it was *worth* it to get out of here? Oh, Wilbur, you say the cleverest things . . .

CAN I, MOM?

Character: A small child (male or female).

Mom, can I have a dime? . . . Then can I have a quarter? . . . But, Mom, all the other kids have money . . . How do they get it? They just keep pestering until their mothers give in . . Will you give in, Mom? . . . What do I want a dime for? Well, I want a candy bar, a whistle, a bubble-blower, and a new bike. *What?* All right, then, give me seventy-five dollars! . . . What you mean, I'm ridiculous? Last night you called me a *dear.* You sure change your mind a lot . . .

What's that, I can *earn* a dime? If that means what I think it means, I'm not interested. What do I have to do? . . . Mow the lawn, trim the hedge, sweep the stairs, wash the dishes, polish the shoes . . . you know what — I'm going to join the kids' union! We won't take less than fifteen cents for *anything.*

What's that, no dime? All right, Mom, but someday you'll be sorry . . . You're *sorry already?* . . . Tell you what — I'll settle for a nickel. A measly little dirty old nickel. Just think of the happy expression on my grimy little face as I trudge down to. the store with a dirty old nickel in my dirty little hands. What's that—*go wash up?* . . . Mom, you're missing the point!

Tell you what, Mom, let's settle for a penny. Will a penny make me happy . . .? No, but it will make me a little less miserable . . . Look, Mom, would you deny your only son, your very own precious flesh and blood a tiny little penny? You *would?*

Look, this is Monday . . . if you give me a penny I'll promise not to ask again until Wednesday . . .? *Thursday? Friday? Saturday?* How about October of 1982? . . . I *can* have a penny if I promise not to spend it on reckless living? (palm up as in oath) No staying up late . . . no new kiddie cars . . . no new girls . . . I promise . . . (take penny) Thanks, Mom! Where am I going? I'm going to give Dad the same routine!

LITTLE KNOWN FACTS ABOUT BIRDS

Character: A nature lover (male or female).

Cheep-cheep, everyone! My name is Bobwhite B. Birdwatch. I am here to tell you some little-known *facts* about birds. Are you settled comfortably in your nests? Splendid!

The first bird I would like to tell you about is the parrot. The parrot is noted for his ability to talk. A parrot was once entered in a contest, reciting the Gettysburg Address, but was disqualified for editing it . . . Parrots are also famous for their ability to mimic the bark of a dog. I once wasted seven cans of dog food before discovering the trick . . . Parrots are usually found in South America, Asia, and on the shoulders of returning sailors.

Tree sparrows are so named because they like to perch in trees. When they perch on the ground they are called Ground Sparrows. I once watched an active little fellow and found out his name was Tree-Ground-Tree-Ground-Tree-Ground-Tree-Ground-Sparrow . . . Bird watchers who favor this bird all have stiff necks.

The Nightingale is a famous songbird, most often seen on the covers of love songs. Traditionally, they sing outside ladies' windows on warm summer nights. Most Nightingales are named Florence.

The Raven is best known for his part in a great poem written by a bird lover, Edgar Allen Crow . . . I mean Poe . . . Mr. Poe originally wanted to call it the Meadowlark, but the only rhyme he could think of was *fleddokark*. So you might say the Raven is famous because fleddokark doesn't make much sense . . . Mr. Poe made a mint.

You can always tell a Mourning Dove by his sad, mournful song. Some Mourning Doves have cheery songs but their mates hate them for being so happy . . . The Mourning Dove is usually seen in the morning. When seen in the afternoon he is called an Afternoon Dove . . . If he stays up all night he is called a sinful Mourning Dove.

The lovely Skylark has long been an inspiration to poets and songwriters. You have probably read the epic, To a Skylark, which is the tale of a torrid romance between two larks . . . I am presently completing my own little epic entitled, To a Yellow Crested Barn Owl. Let me quote from my little poem:

Lo, the Yellow Crested Barn Owl,
Lo, the Yellow Crested Barn Owl,
Lo, the Yellow Crested Barn Owl.

He is low because he fell off the barn roof. This poem may someday place me alongside Shakespeare . . .

The Duck Hawk is so named because of his ability to duck when pursued by other birds . . . He ducks into alleys, abandoned warehouses and into the living rooms of lady Duck Hawks. Many a lovely romance has been started this way.

A favorite bird among most bird watchers is the tiny hummingbird. The Eastern Hummingbird lives west of the Mississippi, while the Western Hummingbird lives east of the Rockies.

Cuckoo Birds have a bad reputation. They have a habit of laying their eggs in the nests of other birds. This either makes the Cuckoo a very smart bird or makes others birds very dumb.

The Turtle Dove is often mistaken for a turtle because of its confusing name. There is a movement on foot to change its name to Serpent Dove because it is less confusing to tell a snake from a turtle when it is a bird.

I must now spread my little wings and fly away to lunch. (rapturously) Ah, how I love chocolate covered bird-seed! (exit flapping arms as wings).

GOING UP

Character: Elevator operator (male or female) in department store.

Elevator going up! Step to the rear and face the front, please. Lady, please do as I say—I'm not your husband . . . I'm *glad* I'm not, too! . . . Men's toys? But lady, you mean children's toys, don't you? Oh, your husband is just a great big kid . . . scooters on the third floor.

Door's closing . . . ooops, sorry, girlie, if I caught your nose. Prettiest nose I've caught all week . . . Going up! Balcony—tea room, coffee shop, buttermilk bar . . . no, lady, we don't have a lemon juice bar, but they'll squeeze a lemon in your mouth if you like . . . Second floor—umbrellas, raincoats, rubber boots, snow plows . . . friendly service by freezing clerks . . . Lady, will you please stop that child from hitting me with that baseball bat?

Anyone want the third floor? (laugh uproariously) What would anyone do with a floor?

Fourth floor! Stuffed upholstery, stuffed dates, stuffed birds and other stuff . . . What's that, lady, you want *out?* . . . You mean you don't enjoy my company? Look, everyone, here's a snob! . . . All right, go, but don't come crawling back when you're old and lonely.

Fifth floor! No sense stopping here, folks, everything on the fifth floor is always dropping . . . in price . . . You should see the holes in that fifth floor!

Sixth floor! What's that, mister—you want five gallons of gas and a quart of oil? You sure you're in the right place? . . . Sixth floor—everyone out! What do you mean, there are four more floors? Of course there are, but I'm getting sick of this!

Seventh floor! (confused) Lady, for the last time, I'm not your husband—please take your hand out of my pocket.

(Suddenly) Eighth floor! Eighth floor! Fountain pens, pig pens, pens and needles . . . What's that, ma'am? You wanted out at the third floor? (indignantly) *Who* had *whose* elbow in *whose* mouth?

(Quickly) Ninth floor! Tenth floor! Ninth floor! Tenth floor! Sorry, folks, this car always gets jittery at this height. Ninth floor—same thing as the sixth floor—somebody goofed! Eleventh floor! (frown, puzzled) *Eleventh* floor? Say, does this building have an eleventh floor? (shocked) *Eleventh* floor! Parachutes! All sizes of parachutes, sold by courteous airline pilots! Your money cheerfully refunded if they fail to open.

HOOK AND BAIT

Character: Boy teaching girl to fish (double role). Shift quickly from left to right for each character.

(Boy, on left, speaking guardedly) Well, here we are by the sea. You sure you want to learn to fish, Jennie?

(Girl, on right, in innocent high voice) Is it anything like knitting, Harold?

(Boy, muttering fiercely) *Knitting!* Here, take your pole! (pass pole)

(Girl, taking it, delighted) Oh, it *is* like knitting. But isn't this needle too long?

(Boy) *Needle!* Look, Jennie, don't you know what a pole is for?

(Girl, innocent) For socking the fish as they swim by?

(Boy, groaning) Only if your aim is good. Now, look, you hold the pole like *this* . . . (illustrate) . . . over the water.

(Girl, baffled) *Over* the water? (brightly) I know—for *flying* fish!

(Boy) That's right. Now take the hook in your hand.

(Girl) Where's the hook?

(Boy) At the end of the line.

(Girl, puzzled) *Which* end? Oh, I have it. (Shake hook loose from finger)

(Boy, groaning) Now put some bait on the hook.

(Girl) Like *this?*

(Boy, trying hard to be patient) That's fine, but why use the cheese sandwich from our lunch? Use the bait in the can.

(Girl) There! It's on the hook. (sympathetic) Poor little baity-waity. What should I do next?

(Boy, brightly) You could go *home* . . . No, next thing is to cast your hook into the water. Go ahead . . . (alarmed) Why did you cut the line? (groan) Oh, so you could cast the hook *deeper.* Let me fix it . . . (do so) Okay, toss out the bait . . .

(shout) Not the whole can! . . . just the bait on your line . . . that's right. There! At last we're fishing.

(Girl) Harold, shouldn't we have on a steel helmet or something?

(Boy, baffled) A steel helmet! *Why?*

(Girl, innocent) In case we tangle with a swordfish.

(Boy, weary, resigned) No, dear, I'll just file off its sword. Look, Jennie, do you know what it means if your pole jumps up and down?

(Girl, brightly) That there's a fish at the end!

(Boy, pleased) That's right!

(Girl) But, Harold? . . . *Which* end? . . .

(Boy, excited) Look, here comes a school of fish!

(Girl, singing) Tra-la-la-la-la.

(Boy, baffled) Jennie, why are you singing?

(Girl, innocent) If fish have *scales* they must like music.

(Boy, muttering) Yes, and if you can go *meow-meow* you might attract some catfish.

(Girl) I thought catfish lived in rivers.

(Boy, weary) They'll swim anywhere just to catch a mouse. (turn toward girl) Jennie, do you have the slightest idea what we're doing here?

(Girl, brightly) Of course!

(Boy, desperate) Then will you please tell *me?*

(Girl, excited) Harold, look, the end of my pole is bobbing!

(Boy) It means nothing, dear.

(Girl) Why not?

(Boy) *You're shaking the other end!*

Time passes.

(Boy, sighing) Sure funny, I haven't had a bite yet.

(Girl) Have a bite of cheese sandwich?

(Boy) I mean a bite on my hook . . . Looks like there isn't a fish in the whole ocean.

(Girl, sympathetic) Oh, dear, what will happen to the Norwegian fishing industry?

(Boy, shrugging) Why should we worry?

(Girl, brightly) I know what size pole we'd use for a sardine!

(Boy) What?

(Girl) A toothpick!

(Boy, depressed) Bad luck, today . . . not a nibble.

(Girl, casual) Harold, I have a nibble.

(Boy, disinterested, glumly stare out) A nibble? Well, pull it in.

(Girl, casual) I've got it, Harold.

(Boy, still glum) Okay . . .

(Girl, still casual) Harold, there's a fish on the end . . .

(Boy, still glum) A fish? Okay . . . (wake up) A fish! (look to right, shout) Jennie, you've done it . . . you caught a swordfish! (horrified) Jennie, what are you doing? . . . don't throw it back! Jennie! (watch fish swim away, turn in despair to girl) Why did you toss it back?

(Girl, shrugging) You said there weren't any fish left . . . I didn't want to keep the last fish alive.

SCHOOL DAZE

Character: Teacher (male or female) to class.

Good morning, dear children! Are we ready for our test? No, Billy, I didn't say *our* test because I'm taking it, too . . . *I* already know the answers . . . That's cheating, is it? Billy!

Martha, can you tell me why Washington crossed the Delaware? . . . Because it was too long to go around? . . . (sigh) . . . Jimmy, why did Alexander the Great die so young? . . . Because he wanted to make history easier? . . . Oh! . . . Susie, where is Norway? . . . He went out for a walk? . . . I said *Norway,* not *Norman!* Alice, can you repeat the alphabet backward? . . . No, I don't mean while facing the rear of the room . . . (sigh) . . . Harry, why do bees keep honey in their mouths? . . . Because they don't have jars? Please!

Stanley, if I had a dozen apples and gave you one, what would you say? . . . *Selfish?* . . . Lois, what animal gives us wool? . . . No animal gives it to us, we have to *take it away?* Morton, can you spell *gorilla?* B-I-G A-P-E? I see, it spells easier and means the same thing . . . Doris, can you spell goat? . . . (exasperated) I said *spell,* not *smell* . . . Eddie, how long did it take Magellan to sail around the world? . . . You don't know because your mother kept you in that day? . . . Leonard, where was Napoleon defeated? . . . On page fifty-three of our history book? No, no, I'll give you a hint—Water . . . Water . . . Water . . . no, Mary, *I'm not thirsty!*

Walter, what small creature lives in a corner and is in constant fear of his life? Your *father?* . . . Pauline, can you name three presidents? Billy Jones, Sammy Smith, Eddie Green? . . . I never knew they were presidents . . . Oh, I didn't mean presidents of the Student Organization! . . . Norma, where was the Declaration of Independence signed? At the *bottom?*

Did all of you memorize one of Shakespeare's poems as I asked? Mildred . . .? Fine! Will you recite your choice for us?

. . . (pause as if listening, smile) A very lovely bit of verse; let's
see if I can remember what you quoted:

> I'd like to be a zephyr,
> I'd like to be a breeze,
> But best of all I'd like to be
> A piece of moldy cheese!

But, Mildred, was that written by Shakespeare, the great
English poet? Oh, it was written by Sammy Shakespeare who
runs the corner grocery store . . . Richard, suppose you tell us
where pearls are found. Around the neck? . . . No, no, I mean
before that. In *jewelry stores?* . . . No, no, I mean even before
that. I'll give you a hint: pearls are found in the *water* . . . No,
not in oyster stew! Richard, where are you going? To look for
some pearls at the beach? Please sit down!

Now, children I have some questions that are answered by
numbers. Are you ready? You're *not?* Well, I'm afraid we'll
have to go ahead anyway. Here's the first.

How many stripes on a tiger? What's that, Billy, you asked a
tiger one time but he just stood there and growled at you? . . .
How many ships did Columbus have? *Twelve?* Why, you *know*
he only had *three.* Oh, he had nine toy ships when he was a boy.

How many miles did Paul Revere gallop during his famous
journey? Why do you say *none?* His *horse* did all the galloping?
. . . Here's a difficult one. Marie, can you name the nine planets?
Go ahead . . . lettuce, carrots, potatoes, spinach . . . Marie, I
said *planets,* not plants.

Let's try just one more. Jeff, how many times can bees sting
you? Once, because after one sting you don't fool around with
them again.

(Look at watch, sigh) Well, children, your answers could
have been worse, but I'm not sure *how.* I'll give you one final
question—would you all like a recess? (hold ears) Please, children, my *ears!*

A CALL TO A BRIDE

Character: Husband phoning bride.

Hello . . . Susie? This is Wally. Wally *who?* You know—
Wally Lee, the man you married last week . . . What's that,
dear, you're afraid to be *alone* in the house? But what about the
goldfish? Oh, they won't even talk to you . . . Look, dear, try to
find something to do. Maybe you can wash some of my dirty
shirts . . . You gave them to the Salvation Army? . . . Dear, why
do you think I bought you that new washing machine? (incredu-
lous) You thought it was a new kind of television set! *Channel
three comes in perfectly?* (resigned) Well, let me know how the
Lone Cowboy comes out . . .

Have any visitors today? A salesman? I hope you didn't let
him talk you into buying anything foolish. (dismayed) *What's
foolish about a gold-plated bird-bath?* . . . No, it's all right, dear,
as long as you love birds that much. No, I'm not angry. (rising
anger) I assure you I am *not* angry . . . after all, it's not *everyone* who can afford a gold-plated bird-path. (shout angrily) I
tell you, *I'm not angry!*

Have any phone calls? One? I mean *besides* me!

You have something sweet to tell me? (coy) Go ahead, dear, tell me something sweet. What? You ate a whole pie all by yourself? . . . Well, that *is* kind of sweet. (coy) What's that, dear? You want to whisper three little words to me? Go ahead . . . what? *Your tummy hurts!*

Look, dear. Tomorrow night I'm bringing the boss home for dinner. Think you can cook something special? You can? Fine! *How do you boil cabbage?* . . . Look, sweetie, maybe you'd better open a few cans for dinner. No, you throw the *cans* away. You'll find the food inside . . . That's right. By the way, the boss is a great one for baked pork chops. Think you can get some? No, you can't buy them baked. You get them raw at the store and bake them at home. In the oven, that big white thing in the corner of the kitchen . . .

Do you love me, dear? You did this morning but now you don't know? Oh . . . your mother phoned. What did she say? She called me a beast, an ape, a fiend . . . She must *like* me better. Last time she called me a *male chauvinist pig.*

(Coy) I want to tell you something, honey pie. You know, what I used to say and you'd always reply, *I do, too.* (exasperated) It's something very tender. You know. No, *not, "I want a hamburger."*

Look, sweetie, I have to get back to work. What are you going to do the rest of the day? Start the baked pork chops? What's that, you can use the *stove in the living room?* But, dear, there's no stove in the living room. (startled) Smoke and flames are coming from there! Look, dear, run and turn in a fire alarm. I'll be right home!

LOOK HERE, BOSS

Character: Employee (male) asking the boss for a raise. Can be altered slightly for female.

(Hesitant) Uh, nice of you to see me, Mr. Prop . . . I . . . uh . . . would like to ask you about something . . . something to do with wages . . . What's that, Mr. Prop—do I think I'm *over-paid* . . .? Well, it was sort of the *opposite* . . . oh, you also want to talk to me about my work? I hope it's satisfactory, sir . . . You say I ruined six refrigerators last week? Yes, sir, I'll admit that, but at least it was an improvement over the two weeks when I ruined *sixteen* . . .

I also took time out on the job to get a haircut . . .? Well, I figured since the hair *grew* on the job I should get it *cut* on the job . . . Huh? I was two hours late this morning? Yes, but I made it up by *leaving* two hours early . . . I think we're off on the wrong track, Mr. Prop.

I want to talk about my wages. Suppose we say five dollars more starting next week? . . . What? Ten dollars *less* starting right *now?* But, sir, I have a wife and ten children who have to eat . . . *Why?* Oh, I don't know. Just a careless habit they've gotten into. Maybe I can cut my wife to *six* meals a day . . . The children can always go into the street and beg from strangers . . .

(Somewhat bolder) Now, look, here, Mr. Prop, do you know how long I've worked for you? . . . Too long? . . . Do you know what I am, Mr. Prop? . . . your slave, that's what I am, your *slave* . . . (tearful) Sir, I've worked for you for ten years, and do you know that in all that time you haven't said even one kind sentence to me? I dare you to say one kind sentence to me right now . . . What's that? . . . *Please, dear employee, go home!*

Mr. Prop, why don't you put yourself in my place for a while. No, that does *not* mean you can eat my dinner tonight . . . Just take a good look, Mr. Prop . . . You see before you a poor, dejected, miserable, unhappy creature . . . huh? . . . I left out *worthless?* . . . Do you remember that day ten years ago when I first started to work for you? I was a simple, innocent, unassuming boy of sixteen . . . (shout) All right, so I *was* a simple, innocent, *stupid* boy. But look how I've grown with the store . . . huh? I've grown around the middle? . . . Mr. Prop, I appeal to your sense of fair play, your sense of honor, your sense of sportsmanship . . . What? you don't have any sense at all or you wouldn't have hired me in the first place . . .? . . .

Do you realize, sir, that I am responsible for a hundred per cent rise in the last two years? . . . Oh, the rise was in expenses? . . . Well, do you realize that I have personally increased efficiency around here . . .? . . . You admit that every day that I'm away things really hum? . . . Another thing—have you noticed how everyone is happy when I'm around? . . . Mr. Prop, are you sure they're laughing *at* me?

(Bold) Mr. Prop, I'm going to come right out with it. I'm going to speak just four little words . . . *I want a raise!* Understand, Mr. Prop . . .? *I want a raise!* (happy) You will give me a raise? Oh, Mr. Prop . . . that's wonderful . . . You'll let me work on the top floor instead of in the bargain basement?

VALENTINES

Character: Small shy boy trying to get up nerve to give a Valentine to his small girl friend (double role).

(Boy, on left, sits stiffly, staring straight forward) Hello . . . Mary . . .

(Girl, on right, sits shyly, staring straight forward) Hello . . . Jimmy . . .

(Boy) Mary . . . hello.

(Girl) Jimmy . . . hello.

(Boy) Mary . . .

(Girl) Yes . . .?

(Boy) Know what day it is?

(Girl) Tuesday.

(Boy) But it's a *special* day.

(Girl) I know—I always wash my hair on Tuesday.

(Boy) I mean . . . it's *Valentine's Day.*

(Girl, giggling) Oh . . .

(Boy) I've got something for you . . .

(Girl) Another pet frog?

(Boy) Something *sweet.*

(Girl, beaming) *Candy?*

(Boy) Something made of paper.

(Girl, frowning) *Paper* candy?

(Boy) Something you get in the mail.

(Girl, frowning) A *bill?*

(Boy) Something with *pictures* . . .

(Girl, brightly) A comic book?

(Boy) It has a picture of a *heart.*

(Girl, frowning) A doctor's chart?

(Boy) It also has a picture of a *deer.*

(Girl, frowning) Something from *Santa Claus?*

(Boy) I'll give you a hint . . . what did I give you *last* Valentine's Day?

(Girl) Three grasshoppers and a snail.

(Boy, nervous) Hello . . . Mary . . .

(Girl) Hello . . . Jimmy.

(Boy, gulping) Mary . . .

(Girl) Yes? . . .

(Boy, bold) Will you be my . . .

(Girl) Yes? . . .

(Boy) Will you be my . . .

(Girl, eager) Yes? . . .

(Boy, slump, sigh, speak rapidly) Will you be my partner in a game of hopscotch?

(Girl) Jimmy . . .

(Boy) Yes? . . .

(Girl) What's that in your hand?

(Boy, trembling) My . . . my . . . hand? Which hand?

(Girl) The hand with something in it.

(Boy) That's . . . that's . . . (blurt it) just my fingers.

(Girl) I mean something white and trembly . . .

(Boy, miserable) It's *still* my fingers . . .

(Girl, reach in back, withdraw Valentine, read it) Jimmy . . .

(Boy) Yes? . . .

(Girl) I have something for you, too.

(Boy) You have? . . .

(Girl) Something you *like*.

(Boy, excited) A guinea pig!

(Girl, coy) No, something for Valentine's Day!

(Boy, smiling) You mean? . . .

(Girl, facing Boy, hold out Valentine) A Valentine!

(Boy, takes Valentine, looking straight out) Mary . . .

(Girl, hopeful) Yes? . . .

(Boy) I have something to say to you . . .

(Girl, more hopeful) Yes?

(Boy, again miserable, slumping) Hello . . . Mary . . . (bow and exit)

CALLING ALL COOKS

Character: A cooking expert on television.

Ladies, I am delighted to be able to stand here before you today. You see, I have just eaten one of my own recipes—and that is why I am glad to be *able* to stand before you.

The first thing I would like to discuss is French pastry. I say I would *like* to but I don't know a thing about it. Therefore, we will first take up a recipe for *Spanish* spaghetti. We must be careful how we take up this subject, for it is very gooey . . . Spanish spaghetti consists of a cup of Spanish chopped onions, three pounds of Spanish olives, and the shredded cape of a defeated matador. The spaghetti itself can be obtained by writing directly to our Spanish ambassador in Madrid . . . or, if you're in a hurry you can simply use a few strings from an old guitar . . . Mix all ingredients well, toss them out, and go down to Luigi's Spaghetti House.

The next recipe is for date bread. However, this date bread can only be made on February thirtieth . . . so we will have to discuss pineapple upside-down cake instead. Of course the first thing you have to learn is to stand on your head! You will be forgiven if you cheat a little and make pineapple *sideways* cake.

There's nothing like Mother's Molasses Cookies. *Nothing!* I wanted to give you the recipe for this, but Mother turned me down. But I *do* have a secret recipe from Uncle Charley. Unfortunately, it's a recipe for making ink for dollar bills and the government doesn't like anyone to talk about it . . . However, I'm sure all of you want to know how to make Boston Brown Bread. First of all, go to Boston. If this is not possible, try Chicago (substitute name of any town for Chicago) . . . And so we are ready to make Boston Brown Bread. If you're color blind you can always make Boston Black Bread. However, it's not really a bread at all—it's a mess . . . While we're on the subject of colors, have you ever tried making orange bread? The ingredients are nuts, yeast and white flour. To make it orange you simply add a pint of orange paint. To get just the right color, try turpentine.

And don't forget, ladies, that husband of yours can always be useful in the kitchen. You'll find him handy for beating, mashing, shredding and baking in a hot oven. Remember the rules, though—no slamming with a rolling pin.

I would like to tell you how to make refrigerator cookies, but I worked all morning cutting up my refrigerator in the shape of cookies and it turned out simply awful . . . dreadfully hard on the teeth . . . I must confess my only other cooking failure in years was a molded fruit salad. I set that salad in a damp cellar for weeks but not a speck of mold appeared.

When roasting a turkey, remember the importance of stuffing! The best way is with a spoon or a fork or a long knife. Of course it's still better if you use bread crumbs . . . it saves the silverware . . . I am sure you'll be interested in knowing how to make a jelly roll. I personally just take my forefinger like this (skid forefinger along table top) and the jelly rolls any place I want . . . You can also make a French roll but you have to go to Paris to do it.

Remember, ladies, about the new tangy sauces. Your husband will positively *rave* when you serve him a tangy sauce on his favorite meat. If you want him to stop raving, just remove the sauce . . . What a lovely variety of sauces you can create! Onion sauces, cream sauces, and flying sauces . . . It's always a good idea to serve sauces that suit the personality of your guests. For example, you could serve blubber sauce to your Eskimo friends and seaweed sauce to sailors . . . Remember, ladies—a *saucy* cook is a *successful* cook!

And now we come to Chicken a la King. For this you will need a very large chicken and a very small king . . . If you can't find a king you can always substitute a prince or a duke. Mix well, sprinkle with a cupful of shredded crown. Of course, if

this is to be served at a ladies' luncheon you would make Chicken a la *queen*. Queen *bees* are handy for this purpose.

Next, suppose we look into stuffed eggs . . . (think) No, it's not easy to look into stuffed eggs without pulling the whole egg apart . . . Instead, we will look into sandwiches. As everyone knows, sandwiches were first created by the Earl of Sandwich. Wouldn't it be dreadful if he had been the Earl of Eastern Patagonia? . . . Imagine the indigestion—an Eastern Patagonia for lunch! . . . Anyway, let us make a club sandwich. First chop up a few clubs . . . If you have no clubs you can use baseball bats . . . An interesting variation in a sandwich is to spread peanut butter and jelly on the *outside* of the bread . . . You can be sure that your friends will stick by you with this . . . And the chicken sandwich! Of course you may not know any chickens who like sandwiches so we'll skip this one.

Finally, I would like to give you my secret recipe for a little delicacy I call a Mystery Cake. Primarily, the mystery is how anyone can eat it. And so I leave you with the favorite expression of that famous French chef, Pierre LaFrance . . . (hold stomach, groan, stagger offstage) Ohhhh . . .

LOOK, GEORGE

Character: Wife leading husband through art gallery.

Please, George, try to show a little dignity as we go through the art gallery. Just act like *I* do and you'll be all right . . . promise to act like *I* do . . .? . . . George, why are you screaming at the top of your voice that you have nothing to wear? . . . That's *not* the way I act . . . Come along and let this rich culture penetrate the innermost recesses of your soul . . . how should *I* know what it means? . . . I read it over the entrance.

Ah, here we are . . . look at that picture called "A Hot Day in August" . . . doesn't it make you fairly perspire? . . . (quickly) George, put your coat back on! . . . And isn't that a realistic painting of a fire extinguisher? It *is* a fire extinguisher? . . . Look at that one called "Man on a Horse." How should I know where they are? . . . the man is probably out chasing the horse . . . Oh, George, feast your eyes on that one . . . it's called "A Basket of Fruit." On the wall, George! Not those orange peelings on the floor.

George, will you stop looking at every pretty girl who goes by and look at the art? What do you mean, there's more than one kind of art? . . . Why do you embarrass me everywhere we go? You promise *not* to embarrass me at the ball game? . . . oh George! Please, drink in this beauty around us, *drink* the loveliness of creative art, drink the enchantment of these . . . what do you mean, I make you thirsty . . .?

(Peer closely) My, but that's a realistic looking picture of a door . . . it's called "Exit" . . . what, George . . . it *is* the exit . . .? Oh there's a masterpiece by Sir Stanley Squirrelhead who painted nothing but wildlife. He painted foxes, bears, raccoons . . . no, George, he didn't actually paint the animals . . . I mean he painted them on a canvas . . . no, he didn't nail them to a canvas and paint them . . . (exasperated) George, please!

Just think, George, if you could paint like this you'd have

everyone talking about you . . . what do you mean, if you painted like this you'd start talking to yourself . . .?

George, please stop looking at every pretty girl who walks by . . . (weary) All right, just look at those who *stand still* . . .

(Excited) Oh, George, here's the modern art section. I really don't expect *you* to understand modern art, it takes a deep and soulful understanding of the hidden meanings of life . . . I don't understand it too well, either, I just read that in the guide booklet . . . You see, George, every little movement has a meaning . . . what's that, you *do* understand that every movement has a meaning? (shout) George, why are you waving to that pretty girl? Please pay attention to the movement on the paintings . . . You see, George, in modern art you must stand back, study the picture, close your eyes, and meditate. You'll *try* it? Fine . . . That's it, stand back . . . close your eyes . . . meditate . . . (pause, then snap fingers) George, *wake up!*

Well, now, here is something that even *you* can appreciate. Look at this one called "The Baseball Game." See that player sliding into first base? . . . It's home plate? Oh! . . . Well, the umpire is calling him out . . . (startled) George, why are you shaking your fist? Oh, you think he was safe by a mile!

George, don't stand so close. I told you that art must be appreciated from a distance. That's it, farther back . . . farther . . . farther . . . (look around) George, where are you . . .? . . . George, you're gone. (look around with realization he is gone, sob) *George!*

COMPLAINT DESK

Character: Employee (male or female) at complaint desk of department store.

Good morning, sir, can I help you? A clerk in the sporting goods section was rude to you? What did he do? . . . He showed you how to use a pair of boxing gloves? What's rude about *that?* Oh, he knocked you out in the first round? . . . I'm *so* sorry. I'll see that his boxing license is revoked. In the meanwhile, you can buy some dark glasses for those black eyes.

Yes, madam, do you have a complaint? Your husband is a good-for-nothing? I'm sorry, madam, but we only replace merchandise bought in this store. You met him here? Sorry . . . Yes, sir, what can I do for you? You want to complain about the gopher poison you bought? . . . What's that, the gophers actually *like* it? . . . They follow you around and plead for more? . . . I don't believe it! (pull away) Please, put that gopher away!

Good morning, madam, what is your complaint? Your *feet hurt?* You mean your shoes are too tight? You're not wearing shoes at all and you stepped on some tacks? . . . Oh, madam, it couldn't have been in this store. This is a tax-free institution.

Yes, madam, I understand—the baby shoes you bought don't fit your baby. How old is the child? *Twenty-three?* . . . Oh, you bought them twenty years ago. We certainly appreciate your patronage all these years.

Hello, sir . . . You want to buy a collar for your dog? I'm sorry, but we don't sell dog collars. No, we definitely do not carry such odd items. We just have *goat* collars, *monkey* collars, *raccoon* collars and *camel* collars . . . No dog collars . . . What's that, you'll settle for a dog leash? But why do you want one just three inches long? Oh, you're very close to your dog and you want to stay that way . . . You also want some dog biscuits? Well, try our bakery department—everything they bake tastes like dog biscuits.

Yes, madam, you say our prices are outrageously high on jelly beans? *Twenty dollars per jelly bean?* Madam! Were you at our *jewelry counter?* Stop munching those pearls!

What is your complaint, sir? . . . You can't find the book department? (Scratch head) Well, the book department is where the furniture department used to be, the furniture department is where the hardware used to be, the hardware is where the food used to be . . . Why don't you read a magazine until we get things straightened out?

What's that, sir, you've lost your wife? Have you tried women's dresses? Women's hats? Women's shoes? You haven't looked in any of those places? Why not? . . . Oh, you're liable to *find* her.

Yes, madam, you can get bird-seed in our pet department . . . Yes, for all kinds of birds . . . No, planting a package won't give you a garden full of sparrows, robins, and mockingbirds . . . But, if you plan to have sea-gulls be sure to give them plenty of water.

What's that, you bought a pair of snowshoes and it hasn't snowed once all winter? You bought a rain coat and it hasn't rained in weeks? You bought a windbreaker and it hasn't been windy? Now you want to buy a ticket to Alaska?

SAVING THE OLD HOMESTEAD

Character: **A** melodrama (four roles—Villain, sneering voice; Mother, wavering voice; Daughter, steady voice; Hero, strong voice).

(Villain) Heh, heh, heh . . . old Mother, the mortgage is due!

(Mother) Please, sir, we are without funds!

(Villain) Who's talking about *funds*—I want my money! (point) Go, old Mother!

(Mother, pleading) But sir, the snow is cold tonight!

(Villain, matter-of-factly) Madam, for your information, it's cold *every* night. (sneer) Go!

(Mother) No!

(Villain) Go!

(Mother) No!

(Villain) Go!

(Mother) No!

(Villain, nod in approval) Go—no, go—no. Say, that's an interesting little conversation. (sneer) Go, before I set my dogs on you. (frown) What am I talking about—I haven't any dogs. (sneer, point) Pack up your electronics equipment and go!

(Mother, cringing) Please, Squire, don't you have any feelings?

(Villain, pinch own arm) Ouch! That answers your question? (sneer, point) Off with you!

(Mother, drooping, leaves) Oh, the cold, cold, snow . . .

(Villain) Wait!

(Mother, hopeful) Yes?

(Villain, twisting mustache) I understand you have a very beautiful daughter.

(Mother, scoffing) Beautiful! You ever get a close look at her?

(Villain) Tell you what . . . let me have your daughter and I'll skip the mortgage.

(Mother, alarmed) My daughter! What do you want with her?

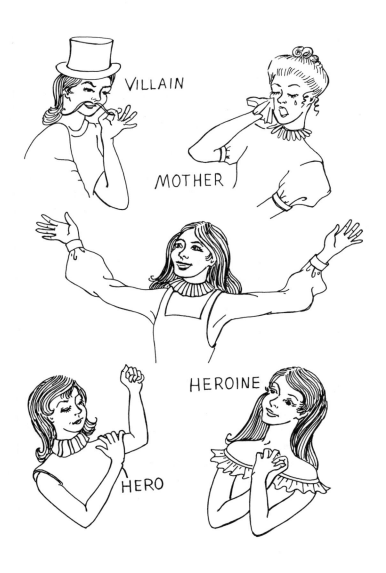

VILLAIN

MOTHER

HEROINE

HERO

(Villain) She can help with the spring plowing. I lost my horse.

(Mother) Never, never, never!

(Villain) I take it you mean nothing doing. In that case, get on your power snow shovel and take off!

(Mother) Ah, here comes my little Nell now!

(Daughter) Mother!

(Mother) Little Nell!

(Villain, triumphant) Ah, my beautiful Little Nell . . . (peer at her) Ah, my beautiful little Nell . . . (peer more) Ah, my beautiful . . . (stare in horror) Mother, is this your *beautiful* Little Nell?

(Mother, shrugging) She looks better with heavy make-up.

(Villain, jeering) Out, out, out! Besides that, *go!*

(Daughter) But, Squire, what will you do with a little old rickety run-down shack like this?

(Villain, frowning, shrug) You got me there, sister.

(Daughter) Come, Mother, the Squire is a cruel man . . . (start to leave)

(Mother) Wait! Here comes Roger!

(Daughter, with happy shriek) Roger!

(Villain, scowling) Roger?

(Daughter, frowning) Mother—who's *Roger?*

(Mother, turning to door) Roger—our hero!

(Villain) Come in, hero . . . I mean Roger . . .

(Daughter) Roger, you came in the nick of time!

(Roger) No, not in the nick, I came by boat. What's going on?

(Mother) The Squire is about to foreclose the mortgage!

(Roger, waving paper) The *mortgage?* Why, I just paid it off!

(Villain, scowling) Where did you get the money?

(Roger, shrugging) Refund on my income tax.

(Mother) Roger!

(Villain, sneering) Roger!

(Daughter, frowning) Mother—who in the world is this *Roger?*

MY VOCAL CAREER

Character: A singer (male or female).

Did I ever tell you about my vocal career? It all started one morning as I was walking through the woods. I heard a nightingale singing while perched on the back of a cow. I listened and listened until I could imitate the sound perfectly. I now sing exactly like that cow . . . Of course this is sometimes dangerous —I once found myself being taken home by a milkman.

My career really got started in St. Louis when I was discovered by a talent scout. He heard me singing a romantic Italian song. First thing I knew I was on a fast boat to Italy . . . It was there I first met the great Señor Galoppi of the Milan Opera House. He heard me sing and gave me my first big break. But it wasn't too bad—I was out of the cast in six weeks.

I'll never forget the time I brought down the house in Rome. The neighbors in the apartment upstairs came down to slug me with big rolls of salami . . . Bambino!

I want all of you to know that I have a very musical ear . . . in fact two of them . . . Why should I be different?

I also write beautiful music. Listen to the opening of this composition, which I call, *Etude in C Flat Major for Trombone and Xylophone.* (Hum a single, short note) . . . As soon as I add the rest of the notes I'll have a big hit.

But back to my vocal career. As you know, voices have various classifications. There are contraltos, tenors, baritones, sopranos and basses. My voice has a classification all its own . . . I am known as a bull-moose soprano. I also have a nickname. They call me, *Clump-clump, the boy (or girl) with a voice that sounds like a girl (or boy).*

I am also what you might call a shower soprano. I just love to drown my voice in the sound of running water.

Probably my biggest success came at the South Dakota Open Air Festival. There were contestants from every state except

South Dakota . . . It was held in Illinois . . . But there I was, perched on a huge brown rock in the middle of a prairie. I started to sing. The wheat started to sway . . . Then the earth rumbled and opened up . . . What an earthquake! . . . I wouldn't say that I won third prize. I wouldn't say that I won second prize. I wouldn't even say that I won first prize. To tell the truth, I was disqualified for using a cheap tin whistle on the high notes.

Another great triumph of mine was on television. I brought out the deeper emotions of millions of viewers. They laughed, cried, and hysterically called the broadcasting station.

I have also made a few records. Maybe you have heard of my recording called, *Come Back to Texas Where the Longhorns Grow and the Little Spanish Señorita Waits Beside the Old Garden Wall in the Pale Moonlight with Sweet Guitars Strumming Down Where the Mississippi Flows* . . . This song could have been a big hit except for one thing—everyone hated it!

Like all great careers, mine came to a triumphant end. Ah, how well I remember that lovely spring evening in August. I sang that old favorite, *It's a Long Long Way to Tipperary*. Five Irish cops marched up on that stage and started carrying me home . . . It seems they didn't want to take me home, though . . . they wanted to send me to Tipperary.

CALLING ALL SPIES

Character: Army officer on telephone.

Hello, operator, I want Army Intelligence . . . Hello, Army Intelligence? What? *The Naval Supply Depot?* . . . Operator, I want Army Intelligence . . . hello . . . is this . . .? No, I do *not* want the submarine base at San Diego . . . Operator, please, Army Intelligence . . . hello, hello, is this the . . . (frown) Who wants the Twenty-Third Pursuit Squadron! . . . Operator, could you please . . . (think slyly) Operator, could I speak to Senor Antonio Moreno in Rio de Janeiro . . . (pause, then happily) Hello, Army Intelligence! Thank you!

Hello, who is this speaking? *Operator G-Three?* Who else is around there? F-Eight, J-Six, O-Five and Eddie Smith? . . . Better check that Eddie Smith—sounds like a phony name . . . I'd like to speak to B-4, please. What do you mean, *before* what? . . . I want *Operator B-4.* What's that, he's going under an assumed name? Oh, 4-B. All right, let me talk to him . . .

Hello, 4-B? This is Colonel Greep . . . What's that, you want the secret password? (think) Let's see, now, it's a state of the union . . . don't tell me. South Dakota . . .? South Carolina . . .? (scowl) *South America?* Look here, 4-B, I want a full report from you. How big is the enemy's fleet? What's that—size 12, double A? . . . Look, I said *fleet,* not *feet* . . . How many *ships* does the admiral have? I said *ships,* not *hips!* . . . Did you find out how many guns he has? Great, let me write it down . . . go ahead . . . five *guns* and six *daughters* . . . please . . .

Were you able to find out what the enemy troops are doing? They're having *rifle training?* They've already trained fifteen thousand rifles to walk! . . . Fantastic! Tell me, are the enemy soldiers brave? They let hand grenades go off in their mouth! . . . But doesn't that hurt? Oh, a small aspirin tablet is attached to each grenade . . . How good are their flyers? They fly just like eagles? How is that possible? Oh, they *are eagles* . . . How many

submarines do they have? One hundred and three? But we sank
one-hundred of them yesterday! Oh, I see, all but three were
ours . . . Remind me to send a note to the camouflage department.

Now, then, I want you to contact a female spy known as
Little Mary. She's six feet tall and weighs three hundred pounds
. . . Yes, she's called Little Mary because her sister is *twice* that
big . . . I want you to contact Little Mary and give her the following secret message. (quote) *Please return my medals, I know
all about you and that Lieutenant* . . . Also please take a letter
to Lieutenant Albert Morrison. (quote) *Dear former Captain
Morrison: How does it feel to be booted downstairs? Yours
privately—Colonel Greep.*

Are you there, 4-B? I want you to sneak into the enemy lines
and bring back a prisoner. You already have? Fine! What's his
name? *Her* name is now *Mrs. B-4?* . . . What did I tell you
about marrying on the job? Well, maybe a wife *would* be useful
in your work—she can wash and iron your secret messages.

Speaking of secret messages, what happened to that message

I told you to send me in invisible ink? I couldn't find it anywhere. What do you mean—*invisible paper,* too? . . . And the next time you send a secret message don't hide it in my pancake batter. Three more bites and we would have lost the war . . . Another thing, I don't mind your hiding them in the refrigerator but please keep your grimy hands off the baked ham.

Here's your next assignment and I want you to follow orders very carefully. You are to make a time bomb that will go off at exactly three o'clock. (look at watch) It is now five minutes to three . . . I want you to plant this bomb in the apple orchard down the street. No, there are no troops there but I thought a little apple sauce would go well for dinner . . . Exactly three o'clock. Go ahead, I'll wait . . . (hum idly) Ta, ta, ta, ta . . . Hello, hello, are you there, 4-B? What do you mean—BOOM? (reflectively) Hmmm, guess that wasn't you.

(Frantically into phone) Hello, 4-B, hello, hello, hello . . . (sadly hang up, again dial) Hello, is this the Spy Replacement Center? I'd like to have a good operator sent up at once. I can have my choice of S-Nine, C-Seven, or Lulubelle Jones? Send up Lulubelle Jones, she sounds like a pretty smart number . . . What happened to 4-B? Oh, he made a big mistake. He *trusted* me. Well, that's life . . . If he ever shows up tell him I've been transferred to the infantry . . . tell him anything . . . just don't tell him where I live . . . thanks.

WHERE'S THE BIRDIE?

Character: A photographer trying to take a picture of a small boy (double role).

(As Photographer, smile at Boy opposite you, speak baby-talk) Is my itty bitty boy ready to have his itty bitty picture taken?
(As Boy, go to opposite position, shrug, speak to audience) Get *him!*
(Photographer) All, righty, let's relax!
(Boy, letting body, head, arms droop) Like this?
(Photographer, impatient) Come now, you can do better than *that.*
(Boy, drooping even farther) This better?
(Photographer, impatient) Come now, watch the birdie.
(Boy, looking wonderingly around) *What* birdie?
(Photographer) The *imaginary* birdie.
(Boy) Never heard it. Only birdies I know are *eagle* birdie and *canary* birdie.
(Photographer) Come now, stand real still . . .
(Boy) Like this? (wriggle wildly)
(Photographer, angrily mock wild antics of Boy) No, not like *this.* (stand still) Like *this* . . . that's right . . . Remember, we want a picture that will make everyone proud of you. *Smile!*
(Boy, dizzy grin) How's this for a smile?
(Photographer, scowling) No!
(Boy, another dizzy grin) How's *this?*
(Photographer) Definitely not! Please, young man . . . how do you look when someone gives you a candy bar?
(Boy, eager, wide eyes, tongue hanging out) Like *this!*
(Photographer, sighing) Maybe you'd better sit in that chair . . .
(Boy, sitting backwards on chair) When I'm bad I have to sit like this in the corner!
(Photographer) Let's pretend you're good for now . . . (sigh;

hold head) And I *do* mean *pretend*. (think, get idea) I know, let's imagine that this picture is for your best girl. You *do* have a best girl, don't you?

(Boy, grinning, hold up six fingers) *Six!*

(Photographer) Then let's pretend this is for your six best girls. Ready?

(Boy, putting thumbs in ears, wiggle fingers) Ready.

(Photographer, sigh) Little man, do you think that would make a good picture for your girls.

(Boy, shrugging) Well, it would be good *and* funny!

(Photographer) Well, let's pretend that you're holding your dog. You do have a dog, don't you?

(Boy) Yep!

(Photographer) Okay, you're holding your dog. Go ahead.

(Boy, arms out, knees bent as if holding an immense and heavy dog)

(Photographer, baffled) You're holding your *dog?*

(Boy, hold pose, shrugging) Sure, my Great Dane!

(Photographer, sighing) Maybe we'd better let you hold a smaller pet. Go ahead.

(Boy, wiggling hands about) Okay.

(Photographer) What kind of a pet is *that?*

(Boy) A goldfish!

(Photographer, with bright idea) I know! Pretend that a bumble bee is buzzing around your head and you have to stand real still.

(Boy, closing eyes, standing tightly still) Like this?

(Photographer, delighted) That's right! *Ready?*

(Boy, jumping, yell) Ouch!

(Photographer, baffled) What happened?

(Boy, innocent) Ever get stung by a bee?

(Photographer, sighing) Young man, why didn't your mother come with you?

(Boy, shrugging) She said she couldn't go through *this* again.

(Photographer) Little man, suppose we pretend that you're playing baseball. Stand up to the plate and smile.

(Boy, taking batting stance) Like *this?*

(Photographer) That's fine! Smile!

(Boy, scowling) I can't smile.

(Photographer) Why not?

(Boy) I think I'm going to strike out.

(Photographer, weary with it all) Pretend you're going to hit a home run. Okay?

(Boy, smiling) Okay!

(Photographer) Ready?

(Boy, smiling) Ready!

(Photographer, smiling) Hold it!

(Boy, runs in small circle)

(Photographer, sobbing) You mean . . .?

(Boy, smiling) Sure . . . a home run!

(Photographer) You win. (bow, exit)

AROUND THE WORLD IN FOUR MINUTES

Character: A travel lecturer (male or female).

Ladies and gentlemen, I would like to take you with me on a little journey around the world . . . but I can't afford it . . . So instead, let us travel on the magic wings of our imaginations. You folks with weak imaginations can follow along by ox-cart.

First of all, let me tell you of some of my little journeys. You know what a little journey is, don't you? . . . a flea falling off a bald man's hair . . . First of all I went to Sunny Brazil. I *had* to go to Sunny Brazil . . . Sunny Brazil was the girl from whom I had to borrow the money for the trip. A grand old girl . . .

Then I was ready to sail. But not quite. I had forgotten something . . . my ticket . . . When the captain found I had stowed away in the lifeboat, he threw me off. But I tried again. This time I was five miles out before they spotted me. I met several friendly sharks on the swim back to shore.

And then I arrived in Tahiti. To some folks Tahiti means mystery and romance. To me it always meant staying after school until I could locate it on the map . . . The people of Tahiti have a curious custom . . . they drink water by standing with their faces upturned to the rain . . . That's true . . . And then my wandering shoes went to Holland. Just my shoes went— the rest of me couldn't afford it. Funniest sight you ever saw— a pair of wooden shoes idly wandering along the dikes.

Then I went to Egypt. As you probably know, Egypt is famous for its pyramids. Do you know why they are called pyramids? Well . . . because . . . they are *shaped* like pyramids . . . Nothing is as romantic a name as a pyramid . . .

The next nation in our itinerary is Afghanistan. Have you folks who were left in Tahiti caught up with us yet? . . . Actually, I know nothing about Afghanistan except that it is a land of fabulous scenery. When you don't know anything about a country you can always safely state that it is a land of fabulous scenery . . . except for Turkey which is a land of *amazing* scenery . . . And Patagonia which is a funny land any way you look at it.

We now visit China where we see the Great Wall of China. They first thought of calling it the Small Wall because in China they always understate things. But they found that it was great. The Great Wall was built to keep out invading tribes—Apaches, Navahos, Cherokees . . . no, I'm in the wrong country . . . But the invaders were too smart. Instead of trying to climb over the wall, they brought up battering rams. The rams butted and butted against the wall until it fell down . . . but the rams were disgusted by the whole thing . . . they went back in disgust to the sheep farm where they had their horns repaired . . . The Great Wall of China is still in existence today. A famous spaceship expert once said that it is the only man-made object on earth that can be seen from the moon. We'll have to take his word for it because he hasn't been seen since the last full moon.

From China we jump to India. Are you jumping with me? You elderly people past twenty-one just hobble behind. Say hello to those folks still in Tahiti. India is sometimes called the land of fabulous scenery . . . and so we hop to Friendly Portugal. However, there *is* a certain section of Portugal where everyone hates everyone else. The people who live there are called Friendly Soreheads. And so we leave Portugal . . . sometimes called the land of Mixed Emotions.

Have you ever heard of the tiny island kingdom of Queenamenta? No? Well, neither have I.

Shrouded in mystery and romance . . . and sand . . . is the desert country of Arabia. As you may know, the tents are covered by sand, the trees are covered by sand, the sand is covered by sand. Even some of the people are covered by sand . . . The Arab's favorite nickname is Sandy. It is hard to estimate the population of Arabia. At last count there were five-hundred-thousand Arabians and sixteen-thousand sand dunes. This count may be revised if a strong wind comes up.

Our next port of call is Mozambique. This country was named after three men, named Moe, Sam and Beek . . . By a strange coincidence, this place was known as Mozambique long before they ever arrived. The natives of Mozambique speak a strange and interesting language. I would like to say a few words to you in their tongue. Uh . . . *Wiggy woggy wummy wump.* This means, *Please take the knife out of the butter before you pass it.* Another favorite phrase is, *Ladoo lado ladum.* This means, *Take it out yourself.* A third familiar phrase is, *Hippy hoo hippy ho.* This means, *Is it raining or am I taking a shower?* Probably the best known sentence among the natives is *quaggy qup.* This sentence is often used by judges there and it means *fifteen years to life.*

And then I went to Panama . . . well, this completes my knowledge of Panama—the land of fabulous scenery. It also completes our little tour of the world. I sincerely hope you have learned something. I certainly have learned something . . . never make a last minute dash for the boat when it's three miles out!

HOW TO PLANT A SPRING GARDEN

Character: A gardening expert (male or female).

What a joy and a delight it is to plant a spring garden! Not only is it fun, but it can be very practical. Think of the use you can get from a spring garden . . . bed springs, chair springs, and if you are very careful — wristwatch springs!

Now that we've had our little joke we can proceed with the actual planting. First of all, the ground should be dry, unless, of course, you are planting watermelons . . . The ground should also be level. This is highly important so round vegetables like tomatoes and turnips won't roll away . . .

When you plant your seeds it is important to arrange vegetables of different colors next to each other. These contrasting colors can make your garden very attractive. For example, you could plant red tomatoes next to green lettuce or brown onions next to yellow squash. I once knew a farmer who planted green peas next to green beans but he soon went out of business. Couldn't tell his vegetables apart.

Radishes are one of the easiest of all vegetables to grow. They'll grow almost anywhere—sand, clay, just plain dirt, sidewalk cracks. I once tossed some radish seeds into the chicken coop and would you believe it — radish-colored eggs!

I wouldn't advise any of you to try to grow iceberg lettuce. The cost of moving icebergs to your back yard makes the whole operation too expensive.

Carrots are delicious vegetables and they are equally appreciated by humans and rabbits. But humans have better manners than rabbits when eating carrots. Rabbits go, *crunch, crunch, crunch, crunch,* while the better-mannered human beings go, *crunch, pardon me, crunch, pardon me, crunch, pardon me.*

Remember to give your garden plenty of water. If you live in a dry area, you can plant strong onions among the rows. That's so the other plants can break into tears and water themselves.

Incidentally, the cucumber is named after Harvey Q. Cucumber who accidentaly choked on the first one when he mistook it for a string bean.

Birds might attack your garden but you can confuse them by mixing up the signs at the head of your rows. Place a beet sign over the spinach, a turnip sign over the lettuce, and a cabbage sign over the bell peppers. This won't keep the birds from eating your garden but they sure will be confused.

One of the cleverest gardeners I ever knew was a man named Benjamin Broccoli. Mr. Broccoli mixed fourteen kinds of vegetable seeds together before planting. He then sprinkled the plot with French dressing and raised vegetable salad!

You must spray your garden constantly to take care of the weeds. Last week I sprayed mine with five gallons of weed spray. It killed all the vegetables, but I had the healthiest weeds in town.

Many gardeners like to try their hand with wild cabbage, but this can be a dangerous hobby. Wild cabbage sometimes grows *too* wild. You have to keep a big stick handy.

To grow sweet potatoes you can simply plant ordinary white potato cuttings. Sprinkle them daily with thick syrup and there you are.

One of the most interesting vegetables of all is crook-neck squash. It grows so crazily you get a crook-neck from watching it . . . Summer squash is an interesting variety because it can only be planted in the winter . . . It's really better if you plant it in the *ground* . . . If you want desperately to have a squash garden but have no seeds, you can always substitute tomato seeds. Just wait till the tomatoes come up, step on them—and *squash!*

If you'll excuse me, I have to go pick my lima beans. I plan to get at least fifteen pounds. Of course they're twenty cents a pound but maybe the market will give me a discount. (exit)

PEP TALK

Character: Coach to football team between halves.

All right, men, huddle up! . . . Never in my thirty years of coaching have I seen a more miserable, ragged, sorry, sloppy, excuse for football. Football players! I could train seals to play a better game!

(Step from player to player as you name them) You, Gallagher! You call yourself a right tackle. I call you an *old maid!* And even *that's* a compliment! I have a grandmother who can go uphill in her wheelchair faster than you hit that line.

And *you,* Lindquist. You know what you are? You're a disgrace. A total, complete disgrace. A disgrace to the name of your father, a disgrace to the name of your school, a disgrace to the name of football. It's even a disgrace to call you a disgrace.

You, Pickswade! I have just one thing to say to you. (slowly, biting off each word) Pickswade, you call yourself a quarterback . . . why, you're not even a good *penny*back.

Pentwhistle, why did you stop running with the ball to wave to someone in the crowd? . . . You were waving to your girl? Ah, what a sweet little gesture of affection. You touch me deeply. But pray tell me, Mister Pentwhistle, *why did you have to wave with the ball?* . . . So she could see you had it? You didn't have it very long.

Mister Robert B. Batwig, I believe. You might say I am dying of curiosity, Mr. Batwig. You did something out there that I have never seen before and I hope I never see again. Tell me, sir, *why did you carry the ball to the one-inch line and then stop?* . . . (pause as if listening) A splendid answer, Mr. Batwig—you figured since you had run that far that an inch or two more or less made little difference. Quite logical!

Ah, there, Redblack! Why did you shift to the left when the rest of the team shifted to the right? (shout) *You didn't want to be a copycat!*

Wampwell, how come you're always whispering in the ear of the enemy tackle? *You're telling him our next play?* . . . But *why?* Oh, he said you wouldn't dare tell him so you dared.

Tell me, Clapnip, how come you missed *five straight passes* in a row? You missed Smith's, Morgan's, Wilson's, Parker's and Morton's . . . before you finally caught one from Leeversham. How come you caught only Leeversham's? I see, you're mad at the others . . .

Allenby, how come you stopped to tie your shoelace *before* you punted the football? *Your mother says that neatness is more important than anything!*

(Tenderly, affectionately) And now we come to you, Snorkle. You were positively brilliant. Never have I seen a finer exhibition of masterful dodging, superb blocking, clever passing. You were easily the most outstanding player on that field. Let me shake your hand, son, even if you did run the wrong way!

(Again brisk) Okay, men, back on the field for the second half. We have them sixty-eight to nothing—now get out there and let's see you do better!

LITTLE KNOWN ANIMAL FACTS

Character: A big game hunter (male or female).

Good evening. My name is Killer Farback. I have just re-turned from the wilds of Africa where I have been gathering material for my book, Through Darkest Africa with Camera and Bubble Gum . . . For some strange reason, though, I didn't see a single wild animal. I guess they were afraid to enter the hotel lobby . . . But you'd be surprised at the load of animal facts I gathered in the wilds of the local public library.

First of all, let me tell you that the water buffalo is a very tricky animal. I looked all over for one—in lakes, rivers, ponds . . . not a single water buffalo. So I went back to the hotel and there he was—splashing all over my bathtub . . . From that day on the natives called me Water Buffalo Bill.

The Pigmy Elephant is a very confusing animal. Zoologists are not sure whether it is a pigmy the size of an elephant or an elephant the size of a pigmy . . . I took a picture of a pigmy elephant but this just added to the confusion. It was either a picture of a pigmy riding an elephant or an elephant riding on the back of a pigmy . . . Now I take only pictures of flying squirrels with their wings out.

One of the strangest sights I ever saw was a full grown African elephant eating palm leaves. Maybe this doesn't sound so strange to you, but I was in Alaska at the time . . . You see, my compass was all wrong; instead of going south I went north. I didn't catch on until I took a picture of an African antelope, which, when developed, turned out to be a Polar Bear.

You may be interested in knowing that there is really no such animal as the hippopotamus. This is merely a name that we Americans made up to describe an overweight person. It's so convenient to say, *Aw, go on, you big hippopotamus.*

The most popular animal in all Africa is the cougar. Natives like the cougar because he doesn't live there at all . . . Many folks have trouble telling a monkey and a rhinoceros apart. But, fortunately, most of these people are only three years old . . . I once knew a man who couldn't tell a lion from a horse. Funniest thing you ever saw—for three years that man rode a saddled lion . . . Speaking of confusion, you must never confuse an antelope with a canteloupe. One sits on the ground and the other sits on the breakfast table. I tried it the other way around one time and got indigestion . . . Many animals get their names from their colors. There's the Red Fox, the Black Leopard, the Brown Bear. There is also the Purple Cow, the Blue Baboon, and the Green Gorilla, but they are seen only in fairy tales.

Camels are known for their ability to go without water for long periods. I once owned a camel that went for six months without a single drink. But I later discovered that it was all a trick—he kept a pet cow in his stall . . . A camel can travel only four or five miles an hour, although I knew one that could do sixty . . . in a Cadillac.

Many animal names are misleading. It may come as a shock to you to learn that the European Brown Bear doesn't live in Europe at all . . . And it's white instead of brown . . . And it isn't a bear at all—it's just a large raccoon . . . Virginia Deer is another good example. Her real name is Marilyn, not Virginia . . . And she's not really a deer—not lovable at all . . . The Reindeer is also misnamed—I have yet to see one who would stand out in the rain.

The Mountain Lion lives high in the mountains. When a Mountain Lion slides off a cliff, he is then known as a Valley Lion . . . Or, a lion with broken bones . . . Don't confuse a Mountain Lion with a Mountain Sheep. The way to tell the two apart is to put out your arm. If you have no further use for a coat with two sleeves, you can be fairly certain that it was a Mountain Lion.

The last animal I would like to tell you about is the mink. The mink leads a miserable life for he is always being pursued . . . not by tigers or wildcats, but by ladies who need something to wear in winter.

A TICKET TO TEXAS

Character: Female (or male) phoning travel bureau.

Hello, Acme Travel Service? I'd like to take a quiet, inexpensive, three-month trip around the world . . . (surprised) So would *you?* Please, sir, be *serious* . . . You're *Harry?* Look, Harry, I'd like to travel some place where there are trees, lakes, birds, squirrels . . . no, I went to the *park* on my last lunch hour . . . I want to *lose* myself in the grandeur of nature . . . no, I will not just *lose* myself. All I want is a little peace and quiet . . . what's that, stand in a corner at the local library? Please!

Tell me about some warm places . . . Mexico . . . Cuba . . . Brazil . . . (amazed) *Alaska? How can you get warm in Alaska?* Take a Saturday night bath? I see . . . I want to go to *Valgonia!* What's that, you've never heard of the place? Funny thing— neither have I.

Tell me, what is there to see in South America? Mostly South Americans? Then I suppose I would see Central Americans in Central America . . . No? why not? They've all moved to *North America?* . . . How people do get around these days! How about something out west? . . . West Virginia? That's *east!* Oh, you can't tell one direction from another. Say, how about a trip to Panama? No, I am not *inviting* you . . . What's the best way to take a quick trip around the world? . . . Place a map on the floor and roll over it? . . . But wouldn't the Rocky Mountains *hurt?*

Tell me, is Yellowstone National Park a friendly place? Some of the friendliest bears in the world are there? How about the people? Who wants *people* when the *bears* are so pleasant? . . . Tell me everything you know about the Grand Canyon. It's simply *grand?* . . . Maybe you'd just better tell me something about the Carlsbad Caverns. It's loaded with *bats?* Why go so far to see a baseball game? . . . Exactly where *are* the Carlsbad Caverns? *Underground?* . . . How do we get down into it? On the backs of large bats? . . . I think you're *silly*. Oh, you're *Harry,* that's right . . .

Do you have anything going to Texas? . . . a freight loaded with oil pipes? Please! How much are tickets? Plane fare to Peru is two-hundred . . . train fare to Canada is one-hundred . . . bus fare to Arizona is eighty dollars . . . How come it's only fifty cents by train to Texas? Because everyone comes and goes by *Cadillac?* How much to Niagara Falls? Fifty dollars, but you can shave it a little if I just take a quick peek? . . . Never mind, I'll stay home and watch my dripping faucet.

I understand that South Sea natives have quaint names . . . huh? . . . *Bobby* Quaint, *Mary* Quaint, *Eddie* Quaint . . . Tell me, do coconuts grow in the South Seas? Not in the seas—on the land! . . . Is it true that you can lie on your back and reach up to pick a coconut? Only if your arms are fifteen feet long? . . .

I'm discouraged . . . and you're *Harry?* . . . I know . . . Harry, I'll give you another chance to sell me a ticket. I didn't say *cricket* . . . I have plenty in my backyard for *free* . . . noisy little creatures . . . What? You have a first-class ticket to a dog show? But I have a *cat.* No, I will *not* teach it to bark.

What I really want is a place where it's warm and the air smells sweet. What!—just bake an apple pie and stick my head in the oven? You certainly are a funny travel service. (surprised) This is *not* the travel service—this is the Apex Glue Works? Then why did you talk to me all this time? . . .? . . . Oh, your hand is stuck to the phone! . . . Good-bye!

HOW I CONQUERED WORRY

Character: Anyone.

You can conquer worry too. It just takes a little relaxed effort. Let me tell you how. Take the time I was worried about the mortgage payment on my home. I worried, fretted, made myself perfectly miserable about it. But guess what happened . . . when the payment was due I went to the mailbox expecting to find a final demand for money . . . Instead, I found an apologetic note from the bank saying there had been a mix-up and the money was six months overdue. That did it—it left me nothing to worry about . . . except where to store the furniture when I was put out on the street.

Now take the time I worried about the payments on my car. "Pay up," one letter said, "or you'll be riding the bus." Instead of worrying, I just laughed and laughed about it . . . everyone on the bus thought I was crazy.

One of the best ways to combat worry is to *relax*. Just lie down and forget about it. No matter where you are or what you're doing, lie down and relax. I remember the time I was worried about my golf score, so I lay down on my back right there and relaxed. Would you believe it—when I was snoring, two golfers thought my mouth was the seventeenth hole . . . The doctor who removed the golf balls from my throat said I was the most relaxed person he'd ever seen!

Of course you can always sleep off your worries. Take the time I was worried about the river flooding my house. Instead of fretting, I just put myself to bed and slept it off. I woke up feeling like a million. Then I just took all those catfish out from between the blankets and had them for breakfast!

One of the better methods for conquering worry is to repeat words of strength to yourself. I tried this one time while I was out in the forest. A big bear was charging straight at me, so I repeated to myself, "Courage, courage, courage, courage . . ."

As I ran faster and faster it sounded more like "Ouch, ouch, ouch, ouch . . ." Another helpful phrase you can use is, "Tomorrow will be different, tomorrow will be different." I tell you, this works *every time!* Your troubles on *Tuesday* are never the same as your troubles on *Monday* . . .

One of the proven methods to keep from worrying is to keep your mind occupied. If you're worried about being overweight, think about being underweight. If you're worried about low grades in math, think about low grades in social studies. Remember that golden rule laid down by Benjamin Franklin—*there's always something else to worry about.*

Another good method is to look on the *sunny* side of things. Suppose your morning started off badly, as mine did the other day. As I bounced out of bed, I said to myself, "Suppose you *did* break your leg—so what—you can always hop to work on the other one! Suppose you can't hold a job—you can always get a bowl of soup from the Salvation Army." I tell you it *pays* to look on the sunny side.

There are also some things that you should *not* do when worrying. For example, never throw yourself out of the window. I remember one big business executive who tried it . . . he ended up being sued by the city for sidewalk repairs . . . Another executive thought he could solve all his problems by running away to Mexico. What happened . . .? Indigestion from all that spicy food.

Another thing you should not do is pace the floor. I know a man who paced and paced until he wore a hole right in the middle of the living room carpet. I remember my pacing days. First I paced the floor. As my troubles grew, I started pacing the ceiling. But this didn't help—I found myself worrying how I did it!

So my final word to all you worried folks is—don't tell *me* your troubles, I've got loads of my own! (hastily exit)

FAMOUS WORDS

Character: A lecturer (male or female).

(Enter with book) Ladies and gentlemen, after weeks of intensive research . . . between games at the local ball park . . . I have come up with some famous sayings of famous people in history. Let me tell you a few I found:

George Washington to Lord Cornwallis: *Give up?*

Napoleon at Waterloo: *Englishmen—nothing but Englishmen!*

Marco Polo, in China: *What's chop suey?*

Beethoven to audience, before a concert: *When you pigs stop eating, I'll start playing.*

Cleopatra, when bitten by the serpent: *I hope the scar won't show.*

Buffalo Bill: *Did a Buffalo run me down or am I lying here because I'm tired?*

Alexander the Great, just before conquering the world: *What's there to do around here, anyway?*

Columbus, after crossing the Atlantic: *Man, that's a lake!*

Eli Whitney, after inventing the cotton gin: *Just stack the money in the closet.*

Leonardo da Vinci, as he painted the Mona Lisa: *Maybe she'd look better with a mustache.*

Alexander Graham Bell, with his first telephone: *But operator—that's the wrong number!*

Sir Francis Drake, after losing his ship: *Salt water will simply ruin my new uniform.*

Benjamin Franklin, when discovering electricity: *Ouch!*

Daniel Boone: *Someday I'll learn how to shoot this thing!*

Davy Crockett: *Betcha I get more famous than Daniel Boone.*

Shakespeare, after a hard day's work: *Hope somebody reads this stuff.*

Noah Webster, after completing his dictionary: *Maybe they'll make it into a movie.*

King Richard, as he sat on his throne: *Who's the wise guy with the tacks?*

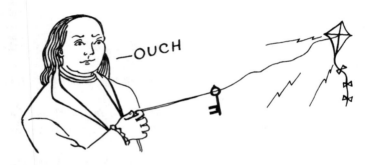

(Look up to audience) And finally, we quote these noted gems. (refer again to book)

Henry Wadsworth Longfellow, after writing a very long poem: *Wish someone would invent the typewriter.*

Samuel Morse, as he tapped out the Morse code: *This is a crazy way to order groceries.*

Franz Schubert, reviewing his "Unfinished Symphony": *What happened to those last eight pages?*

Orville and Wilbur Wright at Kitty Hawk: *Ooooops!*

Stephen Foster: *I wonder what comes after do re mi?*

General Grant to General Lee: *I told you so!*

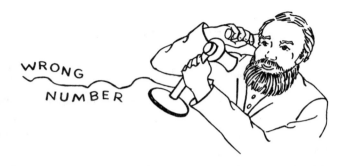

WRONG NUMBER

Galileo, looking into the first telescope: *Maybe I can see the World Series.*

Paul Revere: *The British had better come, after all this trouble!*

Balboa, when discovering the Pacific Ocean: *I knew it was somewhere around here.*

Leonardo da Vinci, after he had been called a genius: *Well, if you say so.*

If you'll excuse me, I have to go do some more research. So in the famous last words of Julius Caesar as Brutus knifed him —*goodbye!* (exit)

COURTESY AT THE WHEEL

Character: A motorist (male or female).

When I'm driving my car I try to keep one thing in mind—
courtesy. I *try,* but actually I think about others things like *girls,*
(boys), money, week-end vacations . . .I'm very rude the rest of
the time, but *courtesy at the wheel!* . . . Yes, sir, courtesy pays
off. I remember the time when two of us came to an intersection
at the same time. *I* waited, *he* waited, *I* waited, *he* waited . . . it
was midnight before either of us courteous drivers got home!

One day when I was driving my all-white convertible down
the street a wild motorist crashed into my left fender. I was very
courteous as I inquired: "Why did you smash into my white
left fender?" "I am an Eskimo," he replied, "and I thought your
car was my igloo." . . . I quietly pointed out that everything
white is not necessarily an igloo. After stuffing some whale blubber down his throat, I courteously went on my way.

If there's one thing I can't stand, it's a speeder. I am a self-
appointed speeder stopper. The other day I saw a man rushing
past me doing ninety. "What are you doing going ninety?" I
screamed at him. "What are *you* doing on the railroad tracks?"
he screamed back. He was the engineer on the Santa Fe Chal-
lenger.

Of course Sunday drivers are the worst. Last Sunday one joker
piled into the rear of my car. I courteously said to him, "Look
what you did to my car, you Sunday driver, you!" "My mistake,"
he admitted, "I usually do this on Thursday."

One morning last month I came across a motorist who was
stalled in the middle of the road. "Can I give you a push?" I
courteously inquired. "Just down to the nearest gas station," he
replied. Three days later we got out of the desert, and reached
town.

Of course, courtesy should be combined with humor whenever
you meet a traffic cop. I got stopped last night and the cop

snarled, "You were doing *eighty*, ran *five* red signals, knocked down *three* light poles! What does *that* add up to?" Quick as a flash I said, "Eighty-eight!" . . . My quick wit pleased him. He even helped store all the tickets he gave me in the car trunk.

Finally, let me tell you of my experience with a road hog. We had quite a race but I finally won. Seems the hog wandered from the farm right onto the road . . . I'll be having roast pork chops for dinner. Trouble is, the farmer got my license number.

If you'll excuse me, I have a date at the police station. I have to write, "I will be courteous" five thousand times on the back of the police blotter.

JUNIOR AT THE ZOO

Character: Small child with parents.

Daddy, look at the camel! What? It's a *giraffe?* With *humps* and *shaggy fur?* What's that one over there? Let's see . . . (peer, spell it out) H-I-P-P-O-P-O-T-A-M-U-S. Daddy, are you *sure* that spells *tiger?* . . . Oh, well . . . Mama, what's the difference between a baboon and a crocodile? A *lot?* . . . Daddy, how come a seal lives partly in the water and partly on land? Because it can't make up its mind? . . . Mama, what's a porcupine? A pig that lives near a pine tree? That's funny, I thought it was a walking pin-cushion.

Daddy, how many kinds of deer are there? Virginia deer, Fallow deer, Red deer . . .? What kind of a deer is Mama? *A Please Dry the Dishes, Dear?* . . . Daddy, what's that over there in the little cage? A *weasel?* Well, it's the first weasel I ever saw that hung by its tail and begged for peanuts.

Look at all the snakes! You say those are just pieces of rope? Daddy, have you ever seen *crawling rope?* . . . Mama, why are they called rattlesnakes? Because they're just *baby* snakes who play with rattles? Oh . . . Daddy, could a boa constrictor hurt you? Why not? Because you're staying on this side of the fence?

Oh, look, there's a buffalo. Mama, how come buffaloes are rich? Of course they're rich. They get their food brought to them every day and you *have* to be rich to afford *that* . . . Daddy, how come buffaloes are so shaggy? *Their barber is sick?* You sure know a lot . . . Look at the lions! Daddy, how do they train lions? They just put them in box cars at the railroad station? No, not that kind of train! I mean, how do they make them sit up so straight? By telling them that it's bad manners to slouch? . . . Mama, look at those big peppermint sticks over there? Those are *zebras?* . . . Why do zebras have stripes? So they'll be ready for prison in case they're *bad?*

Look at that sick leopard. Wouldn't *you* be sick if you had all those spots? . . . Watch out, Mama, there's a big mouse! (peer) Funny way to spell mouse . . . (spell it out) M-O-O-S-E . . . Hope Aunt Clara comes here—look at that anteater . . . (gesture with delight) I see the bear pacing back and forth, back and forth, back and forth . . . (disappointed) Oh, he spoiled it all . . . he's going forth and back, forth and back.

Mama, can I buy some ice cream for the Polar Bear? . . . If he doesn't eat it, I will. And while we're at it, I might as well munch some popcorn for the monkeys . . . Daddy, what kind of sound does a gorilla make? A *snoring* sound? I mean when he's *awake*, like the talking gorilla down at your office. Well, how come you always tell us about that big gorilla who tells you what to do? Mama, stop pinching my arm.

Those crocodiles must be very bashful, they're always hiding under the water . . . Huh? I'd be bashful too if I was nine feet long and had a big mouth? . . . Mama, why do crocodiles have scales? Probably because they like music? . . . What's the difference between a crocodile and an alligator? The *spelling?* . . . Look at that big pig! That's a *boar?* What's a boar? Someone who talks too much?

Daddy, look! Isn't that a cute little animal? Daddy, wait, why are you dragging us away? *What?* Mama might get *ideas?* Just by looking at a *mink?*

HERE, FIDO!

Character: Man teaching tricks to dog (double role). **As dog, get down on all fours when necessary.**

(Man, right, calling) Here Fido, here Fido . . .

(Fido, left) Woof woof woof woof!

(Man) Fido, I want to teach you a few tricks. Would you like that?

(Fido, happy) Woof woof woof!

(Man) The first trick is to sit up. Understand? All right, Fido—*sit up!*

(Fido, lying down, with questioning bark) Woof, woof?

(Man, patient) No, no, boy—sit *up,* like this! (illustrate by sitting up on knees with drooping hands) Get it?

(Fido, happy) Woof woof!

(Man) Okay—*sit up!*

(Fido, sitting up with hands drooping, but pointed inward, toward self) Woof?

(Man, patient) Not quite, boy . . . look at me . . . like *this.* (illustrate) Okay—*sit up!*

(Fido, lying down again) Woof?

(Man, sighing) Maybe I'd better teach you to walk in a circle. Look! . . . (walk in circle) Get it? Okay—*circle walk!*

(Fido, walking in perfect square, make sharp turns at corners, look hopefully up) Woof woof?

(Man, impatient) Fido, don't you know the difference between a circle and a square?

(Fido, sadly shaking head) Woof . . .

(Man, again kindly) That's all right, boy . . . maybe you can learn to shake hands . . . like *this* . . . (hold out hand) Get it? Okay—*shake hands.*

(Fido, happily, jerkily shake leg) Woof woof woof woof woof woof woof!

(Man) Fido, please, don't you know your front paw?

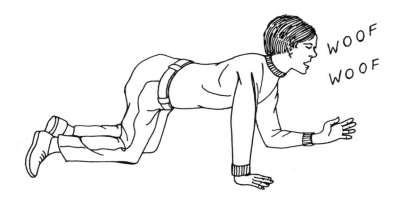

(Fido, sadly shaking head) Woof . . .

(Man) Maybe you can learn to *count*. Fido, listen . . . (**rap four times as you count**) One . . . two . . . three . . . four . . . get it?

(Fido, happy) Woof!

(Man) All right—*count to four!*

(Fido) Woof . . .

(Man, pleased) Go on . . .

(Fido) Woof . . .

(Man) Go on . . .

(Fido) Woof . . .

(Man, happy) Almost . . . go on . . .

(Fido, in sharp rapid barks) Woof woof woof woof woof **woof** woof! (sink down, head between arms in shame)

(Man) Come on, boy, counting to four is *easy* . . . just repeat after me—*woof!*

(Fido) Woof!

(Man) Woof woof!

(Fido) Woof woof!

(Man) Woof woof woof!

(Fido) Woof woof woof!

(Man, pleased) Woof woof woof woof!

(Fido, as before in sharp continuous count) Woof woof woof woof woof woof woof!

(Man) Let's forget counting. Do you suppose you can learn to jump over a stick? Watch . . . (illustrate by jumping over imaginary stick) Okay, Fido, your turn—*jump!*

(Fido, approach stick, hesitate, stop)

(Man) Too bad. Let's see if you can pretend to go to sleep. Look at me, Fido . . . (palms together, alongside face, in sleep) Get it?

(Fido) Woof woof!

(Man) All right—*sleep!*

(Fido, palms together alongside face, lie down on chair, close eyes, bark sleepily) Woooooooof . . .

(Man, delighted) Wonderful! Fido, you're great! Wake up and we'll try something else . . . (impatient) Fido, wake up!

(Fido, asleep, snoring) Woooooooof . . .

(Man) Fido, wake up!

(Fido, asleep) Woooooooof . . .

(Man, reaching down, pat Fido) Well, you just rest. *Good, good* boy! (bow and exit)

SIZE, PLEASE

Character: Woman buying a pair of shoes.

I'd like to buy some shoes . . . How many? . . . *Please!* I want a *pair* of shoes, of course. Do you think you have anything in my size? You think a couple of *shoe boxes* might fit? . . . Now, what I really want is a pair of red shoes with black trim . . . (think) Or, was it *orange* shoes with *lavender* trim? Dear me, I can never remember what I want . . . (excited) I got it! I want a pound of beef liver and some onions . . . oh, no, that's another store . . . Maybe you'd better measure me for size . . . (shout) What are you doing with that yardstick? . . . I assure you, sir, I have *very tiny feet!*

I'm tired of high-heel shoes that make the same old sound . . . *clickity clack, clickity clack* . . . don't you have some that go *bumpity bump?* I like to be *different.* You do have something that's different? How do they go? *Sloshily slosh, sloshily slosh—* but they can only be worn in the shower . . .?

Young man . . . you don't mind if I call you *young man,* do you? After all, I don't know you well enough to call you by name . . . What? that pleases you immensely. Maybe you could show me some beach sandals. I simply *adore* beach sandals. No, I'm not going to the beach—I just like to set them on the table and think of a winter vacation in Florida.

How about that pair of low-heels over there? Yes, try them on. No, no, on *me!* . . . They are *not* too small for me . . . is it necessary for you to groan like that? . . . Well, I wish you wouldn't make it so obvious by bracing yourself against the wall . . . Are they on? My, but that left foot feels tight . . . Let me stand up . . . better take my arm, I feel like I'm standing on rocks. I *am?* . . . this is the bargain basement and they never cleared out the rocks? . . . Easy, now, see if I can walk to the mirror. (stare) Heavens, I'm wearing *your* shoes . . . oh, please step aside. (pleased)

There! My, but I make a pretty picture. Look! They're split-ting at the seams! . . . Poor quality to split so soon! How *dare* you say they're five sizes too small! . . . four sizes, yes, but not *five* . . . Well, you'd better take them off. All right, I'll wait until you can get some help . . . Easy, now . . . oof! Heavens, you've ruined my feet.

Young man, I'm going to report you to the manager. What is your name? Bill Pill? What's the manager's name? Phil Pill? What's the owner's name? *Daddy* Pill? Well, I'll give you one more chance . . .

Maybe I'd better get some bedroom slippers. No, I don't mean slippers the size of a bedroom! . . . I'll also take some bathroom slippers, some kitchen slippers, some closet slippers and some back porch slippers. You don't have back porch slippers? . . . mighty small stock you carry.

Tell me, do you have shoes that will make me four inches taller? Oh, only *two* inches taller. Well, sell me two pairs and I'll wear one on top of the other . . . How much are they? Ten dollars a pair? Maybe I'd better just take *one* shoe . . . the five dollar saving will be worth the limp.

How about showing me some open-toes? No, I am *not* asking you to show me your tootsies! . . . Can you get me the latest fashion from Paris? You *can?* (baffled) Where are you going? To buy a ticket to France? Young man, you are very impertinent to me. Wrap up my purchases and I'll be on my way. I haven't bought anything yet? . . . Well, maybe I'd just better leave with the shoes I came in with. Huh? I came in *barefoot?* Good-bye.

MILDRED (MILTON) MIXUP

Character: A mixed-up young lady (or man).

Hello . . . *gadies* and *lentlemen* . . . I mean ladies and gentlemen . . . my name is Mildred (Milton) Mixup . . . and that's just what I do . . . I get things all mixed up . . . it's really a *meadful dress* . . . I mean a *leadful hess* . . . I mean a dreadful mess . . . I get into *tore mouble* . . . I mean more trouble . . .

You see, instead of catching a train I'm always *tretching* a *main* . . . it's sure a silly sight, me trying to *tretch* a *main,* but it's the best I *tan coo* . . . *can do* . . . And instead of combing my hair I *home* my *care* . . .

It's even worse when I try to *lo* to *gunch* . . . I mean go to lunch. I get awfully hungry . . . sometimes I even have to wait until supper before *faving good* . . . I mean, having food . . . Sometimes I try to nibble a bag of peanuts, but it always ends up as a *pag* of *beanuts* . . . Worst of all, I love to eat pork chops, but they always turn out to be *corp pops* . . .

This mix-up gives me trouble at school, too. Instead of good grades in spelling, I get *spood rades* in *smelling* . . . Instead of memorizing the Constitution, I *consitiute* the *memorization.* And instead of knowing that it was Columbus who discovered America I know that it was *discover* who *Americad Columbus* . . .

In school sports I have an awful time. All the others play volley ball, but I stand all alone in a corner playing *balley vol.* Instead of swimming in the pool I *pim* in the *swhool.* When everyone else is playing basketball I am *basketing playball.* And while I can never hit a home run I can sure swat some swell *rone hums* . . .

The *taddest wing* of all . . . I mean the saddest thing of all is my *lomantic rife* . . . I mean my romantic life. I don't have a boy (girl) friend . . . instead, I have a *foy rend* (erl grend). Instead of moonlight nights we have to settle for *toonlight bites.* Instead of sweet music I listen to *meet susic* . . . And instead of making calls on the telephone, I make *talls* on the *cellephone*. Even the ringing of the phone is different . . . most people hear a ting-a-ling, but all I ever hear is a *ling-a-ting* . . .

Even my clothes don't fit. Instead of wearing a size five shoe, I have to take a *five wise foo*. You never saw a more ridiculous sight. Everyone thinks I have *fig beet* . . . big feet . . .

But I don't want to trouble you with my bothers . . . I just wanted to explain a *too fwings* . . . few things . . . If any of you out there want to talk to me, just dial Winston 555666777. That really isn't my number, but the way things are mixed up, you'll probably hear me answer!

BUT, DOCTOR

Character: Doctor to patient.

Hello, Mrs. Treep . . . what's that, you have shooting pains? Any idea what caused them? Oh, your husband's shotgun . . . (amazed) But that's fantastic, how could he mistake you for a wild duck? *You were flying around the house in a wild rage . . .?*

You also see squares before your eyes? That's odd, most people see spots . . . oh, you like to change the pattern . . . Tell me, is your tongue coated? Not only has a coat, but *trousers to match?* . . . Are you getting enough sleep, Mrs. Treep? *Thirty-six* hours per day? . . . Oh, you sleep *faster* than most people . . . How much do you weigh? Five hundred and sixty pounds? But how much when you're *not* carrying the piano?

Mrs. Treep, would you please say *Ah?* Say it again in a higher voice . . . again in a lower voice . . . again, in a higher voice . . . no, nothing, I just wanted a little music . . . How is your appe-

tite? I mean how much do you eat in a week? Two roasts of beef
. . . a leg of lamb . . . five dozen eggs . . . nine pounds of spaghetti . . . twelve loaves of bread . . . you eat that in a *week?*
(relieved) Oh, that's not for a week—it's *daily!*

Did you take that bottle of pills I gave you? *Why* was it hard
going down? Well, try taking them *out* of the bottle! . . . What's
that, you have an earache . . . from listening to a screaming voice
all day long? Why don't you tell your husband to keep quiet?
Oh, it's *your* voice . . .

What's that, Mrs. Treep? You hear bells every afternoon at
three? Well, you'll be all right . . . just wait till the ice cream man
turns the corner.

You also have hiccups? Try holding your breath and counting.
You *did?* For how long? Well, try going *over* a million next time
. . . You're overly tired at night after a simple day of washing,
ironing, scrubbing? Well, you'll just have to give up tunnel dig-
ging on the night shift . . . Your head spins while washing? . . .
take it *out* of the machine.

You have nightmares after eating sauerkraut and you're going
to eat it again tonight? But *why?* Oh, you dream that your husband is rich and handsome and you like it better that way . . .

I recommend that you go to the country for a rest. Oh, *any*
country . . . you know, France, Japan, Australia . . . goodbye . . .

THE CABBIE

Character: A taxi fare (male or female).

Cabbie, please take me to 428 Washington Street. I want to go to the Mexican Cafe. You know, where they serve tamales and chili and chop suey.

Driver, are you sure you're going the right way? What's that —you know this city like the back of your hand. Who looks at the back of his hand? . . . How much is the fare so far? Two dollars and twenty cents? Isn't that kind of steep? Oh, I see, it's uphill all the way . . . Driver, how come we're going over a bridge? Oh, it's easier than going *under* it . . . Driver, shouldn't we be passing through a tunnel? I distinctly remember passing through one the last time . . . No, I will *not* put a sack over my head and pretend.

Cabbie, will you please stop long enough for me to look at a road sign? Thank you. (peer out) What does that say . . .? Joe's Hot Dogs—Five Miles. (peer hard) With mustard—Ten Miles . . . What's that other sign over there . . .? Hmmm . . . You are now entering the state of Kansas. Anyone caught stealing corn will be lined up against the wall with the crows!

Driver! Please! You don't know where we are, do you? Why don't you stop and ask someone? What do you mean, your mother told you never to speak to strangers . . .? Look, do you have a map? Fine. Let me look at it. (take map) Now we'll get somewhere. Let's see . . . San Francisco . . . Los Angeles . . . San Diego . . . Driver! I believe you're going the long way just to add up the fare. Just for that, no tip!

Wait a minute! What's that big ditch over there? And what's that sign above it? Hmmm. *You are now entering the Grand Canyon.* Driver, you should have made a left hand turn back there.

How much is the fare now? No charge at all? How come? What do you mean, there's no use for money out here?

Cabbie, I'm getting awfully hot and thirsty. Will you stop somewhere so I can get a drink of water? Why are you handing me that shovel? To dig for uranium!

Look, have you any idea at all where we are? No, but you'll ask the first living thing you see? Fine! Oh, look . . . ask over there! (pause) Well, what did the buffalo say?

Driver, will you kindly wake me up when we get to the Mexican Cafe? Thank you. (doze) Huh? What's that? We're here? At last! (look out) There it is, the Mexican Cafe! Well, here you are, driver, eighty-seven dollars and sixty cents. (peer out) Let me make sure I have the right place before I get out. What's that sign? Mexican Cafe, the best hot tamales in all Mexico City. Mexico City? (lean back) Well, take me back to our native land, driver. And remember, no crazy left turns along the way!

HOW TO BE SUCCESSFUL

Character: A lecturer (male or female).

Good evening, ladies and gentlemen. Allow me to introduce myself. My name is . . . is . . . (pull out slip of paper, read name) Ah, yes . . . Aubrey Q. Fliptop. No doubt you recognize me as the author of that best-selling book, How to Make Friends with Airedales.

I have been asked to give you a few *pointers* on how to make a success of yourself in the world. My first advice to you is to *think big*. Let me repeat that . . . *thimk* . . . (shake head) *thimk* . . . (give up) Whatever you do . . . you know what!

Secondly, you must put yourself in the place of the other fellow. Take the case of Robert B. Switchouse who was an unsuccessful salesman for twenty years. One day he walked boldly into the office of the president of Associated Gum Wrappers Corporation. He asked the president if he could sit in his chair. The president agreed, so Mr. Switchouse took his place at the desk. He hasn't left that chair since. How come? Bubble gum on the seat.

Another important thing to remember is to *act the part*. If you are a salesman, *look* like a salesman. If you're a bum, *look* like a bum . . . I recall the case of Thomas T. Tigerfang who wanted more than anything else to resign as a professor and be a great lion tamer. He got himself a whip, a chair, and a pistol loaded with blanks. He walked into a lion cage and five hungry lions promptly ate him up.

One of the most important things is to *believe in yourself*. This may sound like a simple thing to do, but let me illustrate with the case of Milo Millstream. When Mr. Millstream came to me with his problem, our little dialog went something like this: (bend head alternately to left and right with each characterization)

Fliptop, I don't believe in myself.

Nonsense. You are Milo Millstream.

I think I'm Teddy Roosevelt.

Your name is *Millstream*.

Or maybe I'm Julius Caesar.

I'm Fliptop and you're Millstream.

Julius Millstream?

Julius Caesar.

I'm Julius Fliptop?

No, *I'm* Julius Fliptop.

Who am *I?*

Beats me—you must be Cleopatra.

Who are *you?*

(Put out hand for handshake) Shake hands with our **very** first president—Abraham Lincoln!

This proves that you must first remember to believe in yourself if you're going to get anywhere.

To be successful, you must make people *like* you. Take the experience of Samuel Albert Shiftless. For twenty years Mr. Shiftless was disliked by everyone. Everyone except, of course, his dear wife . . . who *hated* him . . . Then Mr. Shiftless discovered the secret of saying nice things. He paid such little compliments as, "My, but you're pretty . . . what a darling hat . . . I love your new hair-do." Mr. Shiftless became so popular especially with women, that his wife beat him up in a jealous rage.

And here is a golden phrase which I want all of you to remember . . . (try to remember, fumble in pocket, pull out a slip of paper, read from it) Three pounds of hamburger and a box of chili powder . . . (in embarrassment, toss paper aside) Ah, yes, here is the golden phrase—*Keep trying!* No matter how bad the situation, you must *keep trying.* I always keep trying.

(Look at watch) Now, if you'll excuse me, I have to go to work. (reach offstage, take broom, sweep stage, speak to audience) The mayor promised that I'll be promoted to head street sweeper if I keep up the good work. (exit, sweeping)

THE TEST

Character: A television producer trying out a young actor, or actress (double role).

(Producer) All right, sir, if you can pass this dramatic test I may have a spot for you in my new television series. The first emotion I want you to show is *fear!*
(Actor, cringe, trembling violently. Note that all emotions in this skit should be portrayed with hammy exaggeration in silence)
(Producer) All right, try *happiness!*
(Actor, gayly walk about, grinning, bobbing head)
(Producer) Okay, *surprise!*
(Actor, throw hands backward over head, stare wide-eyed)
(Producer) *Hunger!*
(Actor, briskly rub stomach, smack lips)
(Producer) *Sorrow!*
(Actor, droop arms till they touch floor, shuffle about.)
(Producer) *Anger!*
(Actor, clinch fists, work mouth in silent rage)
(Producer) *Sleepiness!*
(Actor, palms together at cheek, eyes half closed)
(Producer) *Excitement!*
(Actor, jump wildly up and down, wave arms)
(Producer) *Contentedness!*
(Actor, droop, smile contentedly)
(Producer) *Nervousness!*
(Actor, fiddle wildly with fingers)
(Producer) *Dizziness!*
(Actor, turn around, stagger)
(Producer) *Worry!*
(Actor, hands clasped in back, pace restlessly)
(Producer) *Stealthiness!*
(Actor, tip-toe, place fingers across lips)
(Producer) *Wonderment!*

FEAR

SURPRISE

ANGER

CONTENTMENT

SORROW

HAPPINESS

(Actor, gawk upward with open mouth)

(Producer) *Triumph!*

(Actor, throw an arm overhead, look triumphantly upward)

(Producer) *Laughter!*

(Actor, hold sides, shake violently, move mouth as if laughing)

(Producer) Well, after seeing your performance I think I can find a place for you. Does that surprise you?

(Actor, amazed) *Does* it!

CROSSWORD PUZZLE

Character: Wife to husband (or husband to wife) as she (he) does a crossword puzzle.

Dear, what's a four-letter word meaning the *point of a sword? Ouch?* . . . Oh, here's an easy one . . . *what animal is associated with a milkman . . .?* It must be *dog?* Be serious, dear, I'm trying to finish this crossword puzzle in the time limit of thirty minutes. I *know* I've been at it for two weeks but . . . Oh, oh, here's a tough one . . . *what's a three-letter word meaning a five-letter word?* You *know* the answer? What is it? A *six-letter word!*

Here's another tough one . . . *who was the foreman in charge of building the Great Wall of China? Wun Lung Ho?* How did you know? You knew his *assistant?* . . . I'll bet you don't know *this* one . . . *where do birds fly in the winter?* In the *sky?* . . . All right, since you're so smart, what's goes into a *garage?* No, *junk* doesn't fit.

Here's an easy one . . . what month follows *January?* Why do you say *March?* Oh, someone ripped *February* off the calendar . . . Who first discovered the Pacific Ocean? The *sardines?* Please! What is a word that starts with C, and ends with A and has fourteen letters? *Callaballmalla?* But what does it mean? You haven't the slightest idea, but why worry as long as it fits?

There! Finished! No, dear, not with the whole puzzle; I just have the little black squares filled in. But just wait till I tackle those blank ones!

HOUSE FOR SALE

Character: Real estate salesman to woman customer.

Here we are, Fifty-five Pleasantview Avenue. Isn't that a lovely little dream cottage, ma'am? What did you say? It looks as if the owner built it during a nightmare? . . . Please note that it has a lovely sun porch and a lovely bay window, and please note carefully that it actually has a *roof* . . . Let's go up the walkway . . . watch out for those tomahawks on the ground—this used to be an old Indian camp ground. You say it hasn't been cleaned since? . . . Be careful of that water well . . . it goes two miles straight down. Fine for children.

Allow me to open the door for you. Oops!—no door . . . Now, then, just look around and feast your eyes on this *interesting* living room. See that oil drilling equipment, that shattered spinning wheel, see that artist's skeleton in the corner . . . *interesting,* isn't it? Ah, but wait till I tell you about the floor . . . not hardwood, not redwood . . . genuine *dirt.* The latest thing . . . When the children want to play in the dirt they can just stay *inside* and get as filthy as they like . . . And notice the modern lighting system—holes in the wall. Much preferred this year to windows.

Let me take you up to the third floor. There's no second floor —it disappeared one night. Legend says that it returns at midnight and causes no end of confusion to people who walk in their sleep . . . Here we are, the third floor. Look at that marvelous kitchen—bales of gasoline-soaked cotton. One careless match and your goose is cooked.

Ah, there's the bedroom. Please notice that the beds are attached to the ceiling. That's so you can sweep under them . . . And here's the wall bed . . . wonderful idea . . . you just sleep standing against the wall.

Back downstairs now to the dining room. You will notice the feeding trough along the wall so you can feed the pigs while you have dinner . . . Also a bale of hay in case you have horses . . . And take careful note of the stream running through the middle of the room . . . that's so you can have fresh cool water at all times. Even catch a fresh fish for dinner.

Let me show you the back yard . . . isn't that lovely? You can step right from your back door to the edge of a five-thousand foot cliff! You can see how this simplifies your garbage disposal problem.

Well, that's just about it. The low, low price for this lovely residence is just thirty-thousand dollars cash. Of course if you can't raise the full amount we'll take back a small second mortgage. *You'll think it over? . . . Lady,* you must have *rocks* in your head.

DEAR JUDY

Character: Small boy writing his first love note.

Let's see, how should I start it? *Dear Judy* . . . no, I'd better make it more loving . . . *Dear dear Judy* . . . I don't want to sound *too* mushy—I'll just make *My dear pretty loving honey-pie* . . . Let's see, maybe I can write a little poem . . . *Dear Judy* . . .

> Your hair is red,
> Your eyes are blue,
> I'd like to give
> My pet frog to you! . . .

No, that doesn't sound so good. I need something sweet and romantic, like a big poet. I know . . .

> If I were a bird,
> I would make a *wish,*
> I would wish that you
> Were a flying *fish!* . . .

That doesn't seem to have it either. Maybe I'd just better say nice things like, "I think of you all day long . . . except when I'm thinking of Agnes, Louise or Carolyn" . . . Maybe I'd better phone her . . . That's it, I'll quote her a love poem on the phone . . . (dial phone) Hello, I have a little poem for you . . . listen . . .

> For you I long,
> For you I pine,
> How come your feet
> Are bigger than mine?

Isn't that sweet, Judy? What's that, you're *not* Judy? . . . You're her beautiful sister? Well, look, Joyce, will you just tell Judy I called? Why not? You *like* my poetry? You want to hear *more?* Well, since you *ask* . . .

> Joyce or Judy?
> Judy or Joyce?
> If you'll both come over
> I'll make my choice!

(Hang up and exit)

FOOT IN THE DOOR

Character: Fast-talking salesman at the door (double role).

(Salesman, breezily knocking) Ah, good morning, Miss! Could I interest you in some pots and pans, some ant poison, a bucket of apples, tickets to the County Fair? . . .

(Housewife, slamming door) No!

(Salesman, knocking again) Sorry, Lady, I didn't catch that last word. How about some chili sauce, some shoe polish, a gallon of green paint, some baby bottles? . . .

(Housewife, slamming door) No!

(Salesman, knocking) Did you say *snow!* I just happen to have a bucket of fresh snow with me . . .

(Housewife, slamming door) *Please!*

(Salesman, knocking) Did you say *keys?* I have all sorts of keys with me—garage, basement, dog-house . . .

(Housewife, slamming door viciously) Get out!

(Salesman, holding foot) Ouch!

(Housewife, sympathetic) I'm sorry, did I close the door on your foot?

(Salesman, not hearing, again hop, and knock)

(Housewife, grim) Young man . . .

(Salesman, still knocking) Yes? . . .

(Housewife) *You're knocking on my nose!*

(Salesman, briskly) Young lady, I represent the knocknose company . . . I mean the Footinthedoor Company. Do you know that we have a reputation for never taking our foot from the door?

(Housewife) How odd . . .

(Salesman) Our top salesman has been stuck in the same door for fourteen weeks. A Saint Bernard brings him soup and crackers twice a day.

(Housewife) All very interesting, but I'm busy making a cake. Good day . . .

(Salesman, pleading) Please, lady, I have ten hungry children at home.

(Housewife) How come they're not in school?

(Salesman) They were expelled for eating the teacher's flowers.

(Housewife, relenting) Well, show me your sample case. Do you have anything that will make a good chocolate cake?

(Salesman) Yes, my *wife,* but I won't sell her. How about some Spanish stew?

(Housewife, frowning) You have Spanish stew in your sample case?

(Salesman, pointing to sample case) No, but I have a small Spaniard in there who can whip it up in no time.

(Housewife) Please, young man, I have work to do. Couldn't you come back tomorrow?

(Salesman) Why tomorrow?

(Housewife, grim) I'll have some bear traps on the porch!

(Salesman, puzzled) Bare traps? . . . you'd better cover them up if you expect to catch anything.

(Housewife) Sir, you are a *nuisance.*

(Salesman, happy) Really?

(Housewife, puzzled) What makes you so happy when I call you a *nuisance?*

(Salesman, happy) The lady *next door* called me much worse. Now, look, here, Miss, couldn't I interest you in a box of *goatmeal?*

(Housewife) You mean *oatmeal.*

(Salesman) No, this is for *goats.* How about a sack of *freenuts?*

(Housewife) You mean *peanuts.*

(Salesman, toss happily) No, *freenuts*—we're giving them away!

(Housewife) I'll give you exactly three to remove your foot from the door. *One!*

(Salesman) Wait!

(Housewife) *Two!*

(Salesman) Please!

(Housewife) *Three!* (slam door)

(Salesman, holding foot) Ouch!

(Housewife, repentant) Oh, I'm sorry . . .

(Salesman, groan in pain) Ohhhhhhhh . . . I'll get fired . . .
no paycheck . . . no food . . . my poor, poor wife . . . my starving
little babies . . . ohhhhhhhh . . .

(Housewife, sympathetic) My poor, poor man, I'm *so* sorry
I hurt you. Tell you what, I'll buy whatever you have left in
your sample case . . . How's that?

(Salesman, wipe eyes, stiffling sobs) You . . . really . . . mean
. . . it? . . .

(Housewife) Of course I do! Now, what do you have?

(Salesman, sudden briskness, loud as before) How about some
pots and pans, some ant poison, a bucket of apples, tickets to the
County Fair? . . . (bow and exit)

PARTY NIGHT

Character: Girl on telephone.

Hello . . . Randy? This is Carol. You know, Carol Wallace, the girl you winked at in the hall? Oh, you wink at *everyone* in the hall? . . . I'm the girl who offered to carry your books home from school . . . I know it was unusual but I wanted you to think I was an unusual girl. How did I get your number? Well, I knew your last name was Morris, I knew your Dad was a doctor, I knew he had an office on West Street—so I just put two and two together and asked Millie for it . . . You don't think me bold for calling, do you? Oh, you think I have very good taste in boys. (gushy) Oh, Randy, you say the nicest things about yourself!

I want you to know that I admired the way you hit that home run the other day. You *didn't* hit a home run—it was Sammy Sharp? . . . Do you have *Sammy's* number handy? Oh, no, I mean, what I called for was to talk about *you* and *me.* Oh, you'd rather just talk about *you* . . . Well, all right, let's see . . . tell me, do you have a girl friend? (thrilled) *No?* (disappointed) Oh, girl *friends* . . .

Look, Randy, do you have anyone to take to the party tonight? (coy, cute) You know—something soft and cuddly to sit at your side? . . .? (disappointed) Oh, you do have something . . . your *pet rabbit?* . . . But wouldn't it be nice to have a *girl?* . . . *Why?* (flustered) I don't *know* why—I'll have to ask someone.

I want you to know that I've been secretly admiring you for months. What's that, you've only been at school for two weeks? . . . (muse to self) Then who *was* that big hunk of man? . . . Anyway, all I know is that all the girls at school talk about you. They say you're big, strong, handsome, kind, generous, sweet . . . huh? Oh, *curly-haired,* too. I guess you must get all kinds of scented notes from pretty girls . . . oh, pretty notes from scented girls.

You want me to describe myself? Well, I'm five feet nine

inches tall . . . (frown) What do you mean, that's too short? I'm sitting down! . . . I'm a blonde in the morning, a brunette at noon, and a redhead at night . . . How do I *do* it? Oh, I just *love* all those bottles. I'm an all-American girl all right—red cheeks, white skin, blue eyes. I'm as dainty as a deer, as graceful as a swan, and as pretty as a peacock. (angry) No, they *don't* miss me at the zoo!

(Plead) Please, Randy, say that you'll take me to the party. (sad) Oh, Randy . . . tell me Randy, have you given your heart to someone else? No, it just stays inside your chest and beats loyally away?

What kind of a car have you got? *Really?* But can this horse of yours carry *both* of us? . . . I don't believe you have a horse at all. What's that—bring along a sack of hay?

Maybe I'd better give you my address in case you decide to take me tonight. That's fifteen-fifteen Silverplate Drive. It's the house with the handcarved fence around it. Just tell the guard at the driveway that you're a friend and drive on up past the swimming pool to the front porch. One of the butlers will announce you. While you're waiting for me the gardener will show you around the grounds. Or the chauffeur can take you for a drive. You probably won't meet Dad because he's in Europe lending money to some government. Mother is in South America buying up the entire coffee crop. Money, money, that's all they ever think about . . . Randy, are you there? Randy, Randy, are you still there . . . (look offstage, happily walk toward wing) Oh, there you are, Randy—whatever made you change your mind?

MY CAR WON'T GO

Character: Man or woman phoning garage.

Hello, is this the garage? Well, I've got motor trouble. (surprised) Why should I take a *bath?* Oh, I said *motor,* not *odor* . . . The car won't go. The motor growls and barks . . . no, I don't keep my dog under the hood.

Look, I've got to get to work at nine o'clock. What's that— just stay home and no one will know the difference? . . . Is this a garage or a joke factory? . . . some of your cars *are* jokes?

You want me to describe the car? Well, first of all it has six wheels . . . yes, *six* . . . What's strange about that?—we keep two spares in the front seat . . . It has a motor that goes *bang bang bang* except when go uphill and then it goes *dead* . . . It has a speedometer that goes up to ninety miles an hour, although the car can only go sixty . . . (sudden thought) Oh, yes, the car goes on two wheels whenever we go fast around a curve. What do you mean, that's not unusual . . . ours goes on the two *front* wheels.

Please, sir, can you tell me what to do about my car? Yes, I'm listening . . . (repeat mechanic's instructions) grind the carburetor . . . remove the carbon from the steering wheel . . . grease the windshield . . . tie the spark plugs to the axle . . . (indignant) But *that* won't help! . . . How do I know? I just got through trying it!

Well, if you can't help me I'll have to call someone else. You suggest I phone Lincoln 444555? Is that another garage? Oh, a taxicab . . .

CRAM SESSION

Character: Students cramming for examination (double role). Sit in back of table, quickly move back and forth on chairs for each character.

(Sit on right chair, speak as Boy) I'm sure glad we could get together for this cram session, Millie.

(Left chair as Girl, speak in high-pitched voice) I'll quiz you on geography, Wilbur. Ready?

(Boy) Ready.

(Girl) Where does the Mississippi flow?

(Boy) Between two banks.

(Girl) That's right. What country manufactures the most umbrellas?

(Boy) The one with the most rainfall.

(Girl) Where is India?

(Boy) On a map!

(Girl) Oh, Wilbur, you're so clever! What's the difference between England and Egypt?

(Boy) Oh, several hundred miles . . .

(Girl) Oh, Wilbur, I'm sure you'll get an A-plus. Here's the next question. Is Santa Fe the capital of New Mexico?

(Boy) No, it's a railroad.

(Girl) Where are the South Seas?

(Boy) Somewhere down south?

(Girl) What is the principal export of Iceland?

(Boy, thinking) Uh . . . icebergs, icicles, and ice cream cones!

(Girl) What are the natives of the Canary Islands called?

(Boy) Canaries?

(Girl) What peoples live near the Indian Ocean?

(Boy) Mohawks and Apaches?

(Girl) Name three European countries.

(Boy, thinking) Uh . . . Kansas, Ohio, and Kentucky?

(Girl) Wrong . . . they're in *Asia.* Okay, Wilbur, your turn to quiz me on spelling.

(Boy) Spelling? . . . okay. Spell *Mississippi* . . .

(Girl, thinking) Uh . . . (spell) M-I-S-S-period!

(Boy) But that's an abbreviation.

(Girl) I was spelling a part of the Mississippi where it's very short.

(Boy) Spell the name of a vicious animal.

(Girl, spell) M-O-U-S-E.

(Boy) A mouse is *vicious?*

(Girl) It is to a piece of cheese!

(Boy) Spell *mountain.*

(Girl) H-I-L-L.

(Boy) But I said *mountain.*

(Girl) Well, I can't spell that high.

(Boy) Spell *chrysanthemum.*

(Girl, spell) R-O-S-E.

(Boy) Why did you spell *rose?*

(Girl) I don't know . . . they're prettier, I guess . . .

(Boy) Can you spell *electricity?*

(Girl) No . . . isn't it shocking?

(Boy) Spell the name of a large African animal that wallows in the water . . .

(Girl, spell) H-I-P-P-O.

(Boy) But that's only part of his name.

(Girl) Well, he was only partly in the water.

(Boy) You're doing *all right,* Millie. Can you spell the name of our first president?

(Girl, spell) G-E-O-R-G-E.

(Boy) His last name was Washington. Can you spell it?

(Girl, spell) I-T.

(Boy) Here's your last question. Spell your own name.

(Girl) My own name? . . . that's *easy.* (think) Uh . . . uh . . . that's funny.

(Boy) What's the matter . . . can't you spell it?

(Girl) *Spell* it? . . . I can't even *think* of it!

OUR FAMOUS PROVERBS

Character: A scholarly lecturer (male or female).

I thought perhaps you would be interested in hearing a few facts about the proverbs that we so glibly quote every day. You know, *Experience is the best teacher; Beauty is only skin deep; Don't hold a lighted firecracker between your toes* . . .

One of our most famous proverbs was born when two boys of ancient Greece came upon a bottle of glue in the road. "It's mine!" shouted one. "It's *mine!*" shouted the other. And so was born the proverb, *It takes glue to make a quarrel.*

Another famous proverb first appeared in Spain. An orange grower was crating up his oranges. He piled crate upon crate, crate upon crate until the crates were twenty feet high. A gust of wind suddenly blew the whole works down on his head. And so we have the proverb, *Everything comes to him who crates.*

Another noted proverb was originated in a dog kennel. Their trainer was teaching them to jump over a high fence when a lady came in. "Those dogs can't jump that fence," she insisted. The man quietly replied, *"Let leaping dogs try."*

Speaking of animals, by the way, I just heard what I think is a fairly new proverb. It all started when a road hog was squeezing into the last parking place at the curb. Another motorist drove up and said, "I'll fight you for it." "Don't be silly," said the other. *"A parking hog never fights."*

A famous proverb was first uttered when an Indian mother complained to her husband that she had no washing machine, kitchen stove, or television set. So the poor man went out and invented them. Thus was born the proverb: *Mother is the necessity for inventions.*

One afternoon in ancient Rome another housewife complained to *her* husband that there was no water in the house. He angrily turned on her and shouted, "Remember, woman, *Rome wasn't built on a bay.*"

A chicken coop is responsible for another famous proverb. It seems that a hen saw some choice corn beneath a board. The hen tugged and tugged until it got the board out of the way. A watching farmer casually remarked, *"The hen is mightier than the board."*

A famous poet was responsible for one of our greatest proverbs. He wrote poetry all day long but was unable to sell it. He sadly remarked, *"Rhyme does not pay."*

One old proverb originated differently than we hear it today. It seems that Bill was so much in love with May that he followed her wherever she went. People said, *Where there's a Bill, there's a May.* Someone twisted it around in later years to: *Where there's a will, there's a way.*

One day a small boy tried to rake leaves, but they piled up faster than he could work. He angrily started beating the rake against the sidewalk until it broke. And so was born the saying, *You can't have your rake and beat it, too.*

Finally, you have all heard the proverb, *A word to the wise is sufficient.* Well, I just heard someone down there telling me to *leave.* (start to leave) And if I know what's good for me, I'll get out of here! (quickly exit)

WALKING WITH WILMA

Character: A young man.

I'll never forget those happy days when Wilma and I went walking together. Oh, we made a lovely couple as we strolled along—one of us with a cane and the other with a pretty new bonnet . . . How Wilma could strut with that cane! . . . I was always careful to observe the little courtesies with Wilma. I always gently took her arm when crossing the street. One time I wasn't so gentle and it seems I twisted her elbow . . . I always permitted her to enter the taxicab first. Sometimes the driver would take off before I got in—when I was lucky.

On rainy days Wilma brought along her usual rain equipment —raincoat, boots, toy boats for sailing along the gutter . . . She almost always beat the kids in those boat races. What a romantic couple strolled beneath her umbrella—Wilma and her St. Bernard.

We would always stop for lunch at some quiet little restaurant. Of course it wasn't quiet after Wilma got there. She had the curious habit of thumping on the table in order to attract the waiter. One time she attracted six waiters and the police . . . **And then** Wilma would give the waiter her order. This made it **easy** on me because I could just sit and listen for the next thirty minutes . . . Not that Wilma had a big appetite—she wrapped up most of it to take home to her pet goldfish. Ah, there was a sight —a goldfish feeding on T-bone steaks!

After lunch Wilma would look coyly at me and ask a question. "Eddie, dear," she would say, "isn't it time for *dinner?*" Well, when dinner was over, we'd continue walking. We'd walk where Wilma wanted—down to the bank to see if I had any money left . . . If you have the impression that Wilma was expensive, I want to assure you of one thing—she *was* . . . Once when I told her I was down to my last dollar, do you know what she said? "Let's split it—ninety and ten."

One time when I had money we came to a hot-dog stand. I courteously asked Wilma if she wanted something. She *did*. We were never sorry I purchased that hot-dog stand. We finally exchanged it for some bubble-gum.

As I said, I'll never forget those happy days when I **went walking** with Wilma. But I've sure *tried!*

DO RE MI

Character: Voice teacher and student (double role).

(Teacher) Now, Sylvia, do you know the first thing you must have in order to sing like a bird?

(Student) *Feathers?*

(Teacher) No, no, you must learn to *breathe.*

(Student, puzzled) I have to take lessons for *that?*

(Teacher) Watch me! (breathe heavily) There! Can you do that?

(Student) I do *that* every time I run upstairs.

(Teacher) Now, then, I want you to *sing like a bird!* Try it!

(Student, flap arms as wings) Quack quack quack!

(Teacher) No, no, no!

(Student, flap arms) Cluck cluck cluck!

(Teacher) No!

(Student, in questioning tone) Gobble gobble gobble?

(Teacher) Please, Sylvia, *not* a farmyard fowl. I want you to sing like a wild bird!

(Student, wildly flap arms, utter wild screeches) Chirp chirp chirp chirp chirp chirp!

(Teacher, sighing) Maybe we'd better start with the scale. I want you to start very low and end up very high.

(Student) Like this? (crouch, gradually rise as you sing up scale, stand on tip-toe on final *do*) Do . . . re . . . mi . . . fa . . . sol . . . la . . . ti . . . do!

(Teacher, dismayed) Well, *something* like that. Try going *down* the scale.

(Student, start on tip-toe, end up with head on floor) Do . . . ti . . . la . . . sol . . . fa . . . mi . . . re . . . do!

(Teacher) Sylvia, I want you to imagine that you are making your debut at the opera. *Thousands* of people are watching you!

(Student, look fearfully out, cover face with hands, scream in fright) Eeeeeeeek! (uncover face) I'm *scared* of all those people!

(Teacher) Don't be afraid. Remember that you must be *happy* when you sing. I want you to sing *happily* up and down the scale. Instead of *do re mi* I want you to sing *ha ha ha* . . . like *this* . . . (illustrate by singing *ha ha ha* up the scale)

(Student, up scale) Ha ha ha ha ha ha ha ha (down the scale) ha ha ha ha ha ha ha ha.

(Teacher) That's fine, but I want you to be even *more* happy. Pretend that I just told you a very funny joke.

(Student) A funny joke? Okay. (laugh, up scale) Ha ha ha ha ha ha ha ha (increase laugh, down scale) ha ha ha ha ha ha ha ha (increase laugh, almost hysterical, up scale) ha ha ha ha ha ha ha ha (increase in hysterical laughter, down scale) ha ha ha ha ha ha ha ha. (in total hysterical laugh, up scale) ha ha ha ha ha ha ha ha (laugh hysterically, stagger about) ha ha ha ha ha ha ha ha ha ha ha . . .

(Teacher, puzzled) What's so funny?

(Student, laughing) Ha ha ha . . . that sure was a funny joke you told me!

(Teacher, impatient) But I didn't *really* tell you a joke.

(Student, frowning, to self) Then what am I laughing at?

(Teacher) I don't know. For today's final lesson I want you to *hold a note*.

(Student, cup hands, glance back and forth at them) With both hands?

(Teacher, sigh) No—no hands. Well, that concludes our little voice lesson for today. For homework I want you to practice singing in the closet.

(Student, frowning) In the closet? But no one will hear me!

(Teacher, smiling kindly) I know, dear, I know.

SLEEPYTIME

Character: Victim of sleeplessness (male or female).

(If possible, enter with pajamas over regular clothing. Act as if walking in sleep, arms outstretched. Walk to stage center, open eyes, look around, groan) Awake again, before I had a chance to enjoy the walk. Maybe I'd better try counting sheep. One . . . two . . . three . . . four . . . five . . . (look around for more sheep, sigh) They must have come from a very small farm.

Sleeping pills. (look in bottle) Funniest pills you ever saw— they're sound asleep . . . (Pace) I've got to get some sleep, just got to. I know! I'll sing myself to sleep. Let's see, what was that lullaby they used to sing to us in the army? Let's see . . . (sing)

Rockabye, baby,
In the branches so bare,
How in the world
Did you get up there? . . .

No, that's no good. Maybe I can hypnotize myself into sleep. (poke open fingers toward face as if hypnotizing self) Hokus pokus, eepy creepy, bow your head and go to sleepy . . . (let hand wilt and drop as if *it* fell asleep, groan in dismay) I've got it! I'll repeat the alphabet until I get so sick and tired that I'll just doze off . . . A . . . B . . . C . . . (think) A . . . B . . . C . . . (shrug) I knew I should have paid more attention in the first grade. I'll try *counting,* instead. One . . . two . . . three . . . four . . . five . . . (think) One . . . two . . . three . . . four . . . five . . . (shrug) Should have paid more attention in the second grade.

(Pick up book) Ah, just what I need . . . (read title) The Way To Sleep. (open book) Let's see what it says . . . (read from book) Before going to sleep you must first make sure that you are awake . . . (nod in approval) If you are not awake before going to sleep, you will find it difficult to fall asleep . . . In fact, it is impossible. However, you may find it convenient to first go to sleep in order then to wake yourself up in order then to go to sleep . . . If this doesn't work, you're not alive. Return the book and get your money back. (toss book aside)

(Restlessly pace) Sleep, sleep, if I don't get some sleep I'll fall down from sheer exhaustion. (get idea) I've got it! I'll pretend I'm a cross-country runner . . . I'll run so far that I'll collapse from exhaustion . . . (run about with churning arms, go offstage two or three times, return the last time with a huge ribbon labeled First Prize on your chest. Look at it in amazement, point to it, shrug) *First place!!!!!*

(Give up) Well, there's no sleep for me tonight.

WAITRESS!

Character: Waitress, or waiter, and diner (double role). As diner, sit in chair, preferably at table. As waitress, stand up.

(Waitress, to Diner at table) Good evening, Mam, what would you like for dinner?

(Diner) How about a menu?

(Waitress, writing) One menu . . . will you have it with potatoes or peas?

(Diner) Potatoes, please . . .

(Waitress, surprised) Potatoes *and* peas? . . . You can't have *both.*

(Diner) I said potatoes, *please.* I'm just trying to be polite. All I said was *please.*

(Waitress, shrugging) One menu with peas . . . and what do you want in your coffee? . . .

(Diner) Sugar, please.

(Waitress, writing) A cup of coffee with sugar peas . . . (shrugging) Everyone to his own taste . . . (set bowl on table) Here's your soup—please don't slurp.

(Diner, frowning) Waitress, this soup is too hot.

(Waitress, stirring soup with finger) How's *that?*

(Diner, frowning) Now it's too *cold.*

(Waitress, shrug, pretend to strike match on shoe, drop lit match in bowl) There you are!

(Diner) Where's the soup spoon?

(Waitress, hold bowl to Diner's lips, tilt) Big shortage of spoons today!

(Diner, angry) You spilled the soup on my clothes! Get some water!

(Waitress, pretend to pour water glass over Diner's head) There you are, all nice and clean!

(Diner) Tell me, do you have any spareribs?

(Waitress, carefully counts her ribs with forefinger) No, just the usual number.

(Diner) I'm simply starving for some *good food*. What do you suggest?

(Waitress) Try the restaurant next door.

(Diner) Come, come . . . how are your stuffed peppers?

(Waitress, amazed, lean near Diner) Would you please repeat that?

(Diner) I said, how are your stuffed peppers?

(Waitress, shake some pepper into hand, stare at it) You mean these little things can actually be *stuffed?*

(Diner, impatient) Young lady, will you please call the head waiter?

(Waitress) What shall I call him?

(Diner) Don't you have some salad with fancy seasonings?

(Waitress) *Fancy* seasonings?

(Diner) That's what I said—*fancy* seasonings.

(Waitress, take various seasonings, whirl fancily about, shake onto plate) Fancy salt . . . (shake from high up) Fancy pepper . . . (shake backward over head) Fancy nutmeg . . . (shake while swaying on one foot) Fancy cinnamon . . . (shake from behind Diner) Fancy garlic salt . . . (shake with dipping motions) Fancy poppy seeds . . . (shake with cross arms) Is that *fancy* enough?

(Diner) Never mind. Bring me some pie . . . maybe you'd better bring *two* pieces.

(Waitress, eager) *Two* pieces?

(Diner) Yes, *two* pieces. I'm hungry.

(Waitress, put two pieces at plate, sit alongside Diner, point to pie) Which piece do *you* want?

(Diner) Go away, let me eat in peace . . . (eat hungrily)

(Waitress, hovering over) Yum-yum, that sure looks *good*.

(Diner, ignoring) Delicious!

(Waitress, smacking lips) Oh, boy, wish *I* could have a bite.

(Diner, annoyed) Do you really want some?

(Waitress) Yum-yum *yummy!*

(Diner, pick up imaginary pie and plate, push pie in Waitress's face) How's *that?*

(Waitress, smack lips, draw fingers over smeared face) Yum-yum yummy and *yum-yum-yum!*

(Diner) What kind of pie *is* this?

(Waitress, licking fingers) *Squash* pie!

(bow and exit)

DORIS AT THE DOOR

Character: A woman at the door.

(Go to door) Hello . . . no, I'm afraid I'm not interested in buying anything today. What's that, you have a clothes brush that's *free?* That's different . . . oh, *free* dollars and sixty cents? . . . Ridiculous! No, I'm not interested. Definitely! Is my mother home? What do you mean? (flattered) Oh, I look too young to be mother of those six children!

No, I don't think I'm interested in your line of cosmetics. No, I don't think I need a home permanent set. What's that? You don't think so either? (flattered) My, you make it sound so beautiful . . . (quote salesman) *Honey-colored locks that flow over the head like a gentle stream flows over a boulder.* Oh, you dear man. I just can't resist you. I'll take six sets, one for each of my six children.

What else do you have in your sample case? Firecrackers . . . pickled sardines . . . used books . . . an autographed photo of Julius Caesar . . . my, what an assortment . . . You really don't want to sell me all this stuff, you're just using it as an excuse to talk to the most attractive woman in the block? (flattered) Oh, really . . . I think you're just saying all this . . . because it's *true.* . . . (business-like) I'll tell you what. I'll take your entire suitcase. Then you'll have an excuse to come back tomorrow and say more sweet things about me. I know you're just dying to. (call after him) And don't forget to bring me a case of those pickled sardines!

THIS NOISE HAS GOT TO STOP

Character: An anti-noise lecturer (male or female).

(Tiptoe in with fingers across lips) Shhhhhh . . . (speak quietly, confidentially) Ladies and gentlemen, I am Hushwell B. Softstep. You may know me as the president of that quiet little organization known as, This Noise Has Got to Stop. (let voice rise to normal) We are crusaders for quietness, for there is entirely too much noise in the world. I would like to outline our plan for making this a quiet and peaceful world . . . (refer to notebook).

Motors in automobiles must go. There is too much sputtering choking, backfiring. Motors will be replaced with small horses which are concealed beneath the hood . . . Horses that whinny will be replaced with strong ponies.

Babies will be required to cry only in the daytime. Those who cry in the night will be replaced with very life-like dolls.

Loudmouthed boys will be made to write *I will keep my big mouth shut,* ten thousand times. Loudmouthed girls will be left alone since there is really nothing that can be done about them.

People who crunch popcorn in theaters will be loaded down with popcorn kernels and tossed into a lively fire.

Girls who giggle at silly jokes will have their tongue pressed inside an old joke book.

Diving airplanes will henceforth be outlawed. Airplanes may go *up, sideways,* and in *circles,* but they never come down. This may work a hardship on airports but think of how quiet it will be around there.

Squawking parrots will be exiled to South Dakota. Extra loud birds will be sent to North Dakota . . . The owners of such birds will be sent to Siberia.

People with squeaky shoes will be made to run over hot coals on a warm August day until they promise to buy a can of oil.

We have a splendid plan for eliminating tinkling tea cups. All tea cups will be made of paper. All teaspoons will be made of paper. All *tea leaves* will be made of paper. We figure this will greatly discourage teacups.

People who are always snapping their fingers will be taught to snap their toes instead . . . Not only that, but they must wear thick shoes . . . Folks who snap their bubble gum must wear a soundproof hood.

Falling leaves will be stopped. All tree owners must securely tie each leaf with wire . . . People who don't have wire may use paste or glue . . . Large families may simply hang in the tree all day long and *hold* them in place.

Opera sopranos must hereafter sing in baritone. Baritones must sing bass. Bass singers must catch the first bus out of town.

Traffic cops may no longer angrily blow their whistles at people. Instead, they must courteously remark, *Please, Madam, it is not strictly legal to go ninety miles an hour on your bicycle.*

Noisy carpenters will be given velvet hammers . . . Noisy plumbers will be given cardboard pipe-wrenches . . . Noisy electricians will be given ten-thousand volts . . . And noisy cops will be given padded cells.

We ran into quite a problem when we tried to silence people who deliver lectures. We found them all to be loving, sweet, sincere, kindly, pleasant, cheerful folks . . . so we hesitated to do anything. We finally discovered one sure means of making them talk less. We take a rope from our pockets . . . (take rope from pocket) loop it around the head . . . (loop rope around head) and lead them away like this . . . (lead self out).

PLAYING THE GAME by Christine Poulter 100 step-by-step theatre games that can be used to develop acting, social and personal skills. *"The best game book."* SHOWCASE

160 pp   pb   5.5 X 8.5   0-88734-611-1

SCENES FOR ACTING AND DIRECTING vol 1 by Samuel Elkind An invaluable collection of scenes from major American, British and European playwrights, ideal for actors, directors and teachers. The scenes focus on critical moments, ideas and actions.   176 pp   pb   6 X 9   0-88734-617-0

SCENES FOR ACTING AND DIRECTING vol 2 by Samuel Elkind Thirty additional scenes in this exciting second volume feature material from Shaw, Greene, Odets, Goodrich & Hackett, Chekhov and more!   176 pp   pb   6 X 9   0-88734-623-5

ABSURD BLACK AND COMIC SKETCHES by Peter Joucla The black humor in these sketches makes them entertaining and thought-provoking enough to stimulate worthwhile discussion. Ideal for use in English and Drama, Theatre Studies, Performing Arts, Youth Theatre and drama festivals. Notes for follow-up work are provided.   64 pp   pb   6 X 9   0-88734-613-8

SHORT SCENES FROM SHAKESPEARE vol 1 by Selden & Landes Short scenes from Shakespeare's best! For workshops, class or performance, with 2-10 minute scenes for 1-7 characters.

144 pp   pb   5.5 X 11   0-88734-632-4

MOMENTS by David Crawford An acclaimed collection of duologues; covering a wide range, male and female, young and old. The author has been described as "a new Southern Gentleman of Theatre — A Tennessee Williams feeling but touched with the vitality of a Hemingway."

64 pp   pb   5.5 X 8.5   0-88734-664-2

Available at your local bookstore or directly from:
Players Press P.O. Box 1132 Studio City CA 91614-0132

FUNN
Thirt   earn, simple
enou   ed for major
holid   and commu-
nity g   88734-688-X

MON
Over   ologues that
are id   humorous,
tailor   . Excellent
in the

                                    88734-666-9

GIRLS
Series   s, from the
acclai   . Entertainment   , humorous,
occas   k the ice an
outsta   88734-019-9

PERF
Very   s, ideal for
auditi   l and com-
munic   onologues,
as we   s *a superb*
*collec... of monologues. Designed for varied lengths, ages
and characters. Highly recommended."* SHOWCASE

128 pp   pb   6 X 9   0-88734-122-5

LOOK, LISTEN AND TRUST by Rawlins and Rich

A new collection of easy to use well tested theatre games. An excellent source of highly detailed games to enhance performance and social skills. "The ideal game book for teachers and students." SHOWCASE

192 pp   pb   6 X 9   0-88734-618-9

Available at your local bookstore or directly from:
Players Press P.O. Box 1132 Studio City CA 91614-0132